PEACEFUL PERSISTENCE

For more information visit SneezingCow.com.

The essays in *Peaceful Persistence* originally appeared as "Roughneck Grace" columns in the *Wisconsin State Journal* and are reprinted here with permission. Some were also featured as monologues on *Tent Show Radio* (TentShowRadio.org).

PEACEFUL PERSISTENCE

MICHAEL PERRY

CONTENTS

ACKNOWLEDGMENTS

Editor Beth Williams and publisher John Smalley, with a special thank you to the backup crew: Gayle Worland, Marc Wehrs and Teryl Franklin.

Ben for tending the streams.

You, the reader.

My family.

PREFACE

After the last live show I performed before the pandemic shut things down and you could no longer in good conscience cram 400 people into the Stoughton Opera House, a group of women in a book club approached the merch table and asked me to pose for a photo. Having built half my career on word of mouth, I'll stand for a picture with any book club that will have me, and happily did. It was all very pleasant, with one odd element: each woman in turn presented me with a tin of canned ham, and a knowing chuckle.

Reader, I still don't know. I trust it's a reference to my back catalog. I vaguely recall an anecdote involving my brother and deviled ham, or perhaps it was in a column I wrote, or a story I told, or just something I wrote about pigs. Maybe if I could remember which book the club read I could do a reverse search and figure it out. Perhaps you will catch the reference and drop me a note. Maybe one of the book club members will reach out. For now, I remain baffled.

When I write, I lead with my heart. Even if it's a goofy newspaper column, I'm hoping somewhere in there we'll connect. The pieces in this collection are no different. They were composed during a time of personal and national unease, and often reflect that mood, but just as often veer into humor and hope.

After three decades and I suppose millions of words, the fact that I draw from the heart doesn't mean the specifics will lodge in my mind. That I'll see the canned ham and understand. Even as I edited this collection—written over the course of two very recent years and concluding just about the time the book club presented me with that collection of tinned meat—I was on a journey of rediscovery. When you've written as much as I have for as long as I have, it is not uncommon to read your own work and hear the voice of a stranger.

But as I re-read these pieces, I wasn't seeing them with my eyes or hearing them with my inner ear; I was imagining *you* reading them, just as I imagined you while I was writing them, and I was struck as ever by the honor and trust and closeness in this. That we are connecting even if we never meet; that we have shared time and sentiment across separation and space. It is the marvel of writing and reading; I never tire of it, and I never take it for granted.

Thank you.

And of course I ate the ham.

FLAT TIRE

Something went *whump* on the bottom of the car and a half-mile later the left rear tire was flat. It was raining and we were northbound out of Nashville, less than one hour into what was supposed to be a 12-hour trip home.

We nursed the car up the off-ramp to a truck stop. After years of working ambulance calls alongside the interstate I have no interest in preserving the state of my wheel rim only to take a short-lived ride as someone's hood ornament and wind up a cross stuck in the grass.

The good news was, this was a family trip, and among the unfinished business of parenting, I had neglected to instruct my 18 year-old daughter in the changing of tires, so I put class directly in session, first showing her how to find the necessary information in the vehicle owner's manual. The snag being that car manufacturers don't update car manuals as often as they update car models—for instance there was much careful instruction about releasing the spare via clips and latches that were nowhere to be found on the vehicle. Sometimes, I told her, you just gotta figure stuff out by yourself.

Which was ironic, because I then crawled around on the wet asphalt looking for the spare tire under the frame and then cleared half our luggage out and dug beneath the cargo mat only to discover that the spare tire on our model is mounted on the rear of the vehicle in full view and I was quite literally bumping into it during my scavenger hunt. It is possible this scenario undermined my tone of authority.

After assembling the jack, I told her you should always chock the wheels before you raise the vehicle, but because we had nothing chock-worthy I settled for setting the emergency brake. At which point a trucker materialized and said, "Whoa, whoa, don't jack that up yet!" and threw his own set of chocks under the front tire, simultaneously demonstrating to my daughter that I knew what I was talking about while making me feel dumb I hadn't done it.

The trucker hung around to provide play-by-play until I had the tire swapped out, but he was a good-natured, gregarious fellow, and we enjoyed his company, and his chocks. As we pulled out of the lot headed for the nearest tire repair station, I jotted down his truck number and this week a thank-you will be en route.

The tire repair station was well off the interstate and quite literally a hole-in-the-wall joint where only half the vehicle would fit inside and out of the rain, but they did the plug-and-patch in a trice, and charged five dollars cash. As we pointed the car north to resume our trip, I subjected the family to an extemporaneous lecture on the subject of comparative value, specifically what five dollars will get you at the coffee shop versus a tire repair that gets you out of the rain, back on the road, and will sustain speeds upwards of 73 miles an hour all day long and into the night, when you arrive home to your own bed in Wisconsin at 1:00 a.m., roughly three hours late but grateful in the knowledge that all in all, things really rolled your way.

MILLIONAIRE

I hereby announce that I am prepared to accept a million dollars. Or more. I am told all this cash will not guarantee my happiness and may in fact put me in a downward spiral the stuff of lottery winner legends, but I am willing to take my chances. I think it is important to state this publicly in case someone has been holding back on giving me a million dollars out of politeness or not wanting to mess with my laid-back, used-minivan, misshapen t-shirt, gas-station-donuts vibe. No. I have meditated on it. I am willing to face this character test.

Here is the part where I am compelled to state for the record that my life is rich with bounties earned and unearned, dollared and undollared. I am operating from privilege and gratitude. That said, numbered among these bounties is not a million dollars.

I suspect this topic has been on my mind due to a pair of factors: An email containing unexpected news regarding some imminent and unexpected taxation, and an ongoing customer "service" incident involving the billing department of a large medical provider—this latter experience akin to running laps on a Mobius strip woven from used bubble gum and barbed wire.

The tax thing can be handled, and was only a surprise because, well, sometimes I'm bad at math, and equally bad at estimation. What I expected was a note saying I was all paid up. What I got was a request for additional payment that—while it did not take my breath away—did give me the hiccups. Opening that email was like whacking a piñata only to be showered with rubber checks and pea gravel.

As far as the medical bill, it eventually led to me engaging in vigorous correspondence with someone at the very tippy-top of the executive food chain, a conscientious individual of great intellect and dedication who—based on everything I have observed—the institution in question is wise to employ. However, this person also pulls down a salary that—unless he's blowing it all on pull tabs down at my gas station—rings the million bucks bell in under two years. As such I did not feel out of order politely reminding him that for all his solicitous words, he simply had no sense of what it would be to face this madness with wind leaking around the storm windows and even colder winds blowing through an empty bank account. I was neither snotty, nor was I speaking for myself; we have some savings and some options (among them, his email address). Rather, I was speaking on behalf of those for whom an incident like this would be destabilizing to the point of destitution. Those for whom life's chance equation is not curable simply by solving for bootstraps—that much-vaunted variable so often touted by men in wingtips collecting a government check.

Behold, I am veering self-righteous, so I'll bumble back to silly: I believe in hard work and will keep at it (not one hour ago I split a whole load of firewood using nothing but an axe and my BOOTSTRAPS!). But if you decide to send me that million dollars, I'll take it. Then I'm gonna call my pal the health care executive and get his insider tips on how to stay happy despite the extra commas.

THE BAD DAY

First thing I did today was back into the garage door. From the inside.

I had a number of errands to run, chief among them a stop at the computer hospital. This bit of itinerary was predicated on the fact that last night when I closed my laptop it was working fine, and when I opened it an hour later it was a brushed aluminum paving stone. Ironies abound: 1) I had made uncharacteristically prodigious progress on a big project that day; now all the work lay inert within the machine's dead metallic guts, 2) this week I switched to a new backup system that was only halfway through the initial upload, and, 3) I had made a "mental note" to do a safety backup to a flash drive before bedtime.

I also made a "mental note" to open the garage door this morning. We all know how that worked out.

Our garage has two doors. The one adjacent to my vehicle's bay was left open by a teenager who admirably pries herself from bed and makes it to choir practice at dawn, but leaves the yard trailing a cloud of exhaust, bits of breakfast, a whiff of self-inflicted panic, and certainly doesn't have time to

SHUT THE GARAGE DOOR. I would say more, but I vividly recall stuffing clean socks and a t-shirt into my coat pockets while sprinting for the school bus past my father as he trudged in from the barn having already fed and milked an entire herd of cows. In this case, revenge is a dish served one generation down the line.

So I strolled through that open garage door, climbed into my old van, and—head full of my townie to-do list—twisted the ignition, hit reverse, and ran my rear bumper directly into the closed door. I left it only slightly bowed, although I had to deliver a couple of swift kicks from the outside before it would raise and lower without making earthquake noises.

In town I handed my dead laptop over to the young man at the fixit place. He confidently tried all the Alt-Ctrl keystroke tricks I had already googled in a cold sweat. None elicited the slightest beep. Mumbling something about the power supply, he disappeared into the back room. More mumbling, but muffled. He emerged to say it might be a couple of days. And possibly a couple of monies.

Homeward, then. Exiting strip-mall world to the county two-lane, I heard a clunk. I kept rolling. The van is vintage to the point of the odd clunk being not odd. Plus I had just returned from a brief music tour and figured maybe a stray guitar case had toppled. There came a second clunk. I stopped and got out to check the cargo area. Just as my feet touched asphalt there came the most definitive clunk of all. How trepidatiously did I peek beneath the vehicle, and appropriately so, for there upon the blacktop lay the gas tank, having detached itself from the main frame in the manner of a SpaceX booster rocket only without the fun, fanfare, and government funding.

Forty-eight hours previously I was crossing Wisconsin east-to-west at 73 miles per hour with that very same van stuffed to the walls with books, CDs, music gear, and a suitcase full of dirty laundry, and—come to think of it—my currently deceased computer. Had the gas tank detached at any point during that trip things may have been very booster-rockety indeed.

Instead, the van is in the shop. The garage door makes squinchy-squeaky noises, but it goes up and down. This column was drafted on a manual typewriter. No word on the computer. In general things are working out. Although honesty compels me to say that's the second time with the garage door.

WINDOW ROBIN

By the looks of it the robin had been there a while, its feathers frayed, its talons tangled with cobwebs, its attempts to flap free of my hand listless.

The window is framed behind a door at the top of the cellar steps ("cellar" being an artisanal word for "basement of damp fungal nightmares smelling of soft potatoes and mice"). The robin must have flown into the porch, found the cellar door ajar, fixated on the light through the glass, and never found its way out. I detected it only when I brushed against the cellar door on my way in from chicken chores and heard the light tap of wings against the sill.

I reached for the bird, expecting it to dive away down the stairs. Instead, it pressed into the glass, fluttering and scratching, but only half-heartedly dodging my extended hands. I clasped its wings to its sides and drew it toward me. The bird squawked twice, then fell silent. Its eyes were wide with something between fear and defiance. I felt as if I were cradling a breath. There was a vibration: fear, a heartbeat, or both.

My daughters were folding laundry in the living room. I

called them to look. There were the usual oohs and aahs, the youngest immediately asking if we could keep it. No, I said, but bring some water. She did, and we dipped the bird's beak, just as we do with the baby chicks when they arrive in the mail. Rather than duck its head and gulp, the bird shook its beak, the water droplets flying back at us.

We went to the porch steps then, and with a gentle upward toss, I set the bird free. With a fluttery stroke, it flew across the snow to the nearest maple and locked on a branch. From a bare patch across the yard, two other robins rose and flew to the same tree. None of the three made a peep, but shortly the other two birds hopped a few branches nearer. Then all three dropped to a place where the snow had only yesterday melted. The frayed bird sat still for a beat, appearing shrunken and unplumped beside its companions. Then it pecked at the earth. And then pecked again. Nature will decide, I thought, and we went back about our day.

It has been an intransigent, backsliding spring. Speaking for myself, we've drained it of all humor and hardiness. I don't wanna stoic-brag to my warm-state friends any more. Yesterday I stumbled across a photo of the blue Caribbean and nearly fainted from longing. The sugar maples aren't the only thing tapped around these parts. We're all that robin, futilely fighting toward the sun. Dying for spring, and hoping only figuratively. Above the three robins pecking at what the retreating snow would give them, the maple branches were dotted with knobs, maroon buds alleged to contain green leaves.

WREN HOUSE

I have switched off the music inside my office so that I may listen to better music outside my office. The digital songs have been replaced by wren song, which the Cornell Lab of Ornithology describes as "jumbled bubbling," and your local poet won't do any better than that.

The wren may or may not be the same wren who was here last year. Last year's bird first caught my attention not so much with his song as with the scratching sounds emanating from the window air conditioner beside the office door. At first I took it to be mice or a chipmunk. Then I deduced it was the wren, stuffing the narrow space between the air conditioner and the window frame with twigs. I went outside and peered in: His work had progressed to the point that I didn't want to interfere, although I feared the location—just a few feet off the ground—might make it vulnerable to predators.

Unfortunately, I was right on. The day the eggs hatched, a local cat pawed the naked chicks from the nest and left them scattered dead on the ground. That very day I purchased a wren house and hung it in a cherry tree three feet away. I was holding out hope that the birds might try for a second clutch.

They didn't return. Throughout the winter, every time I slogged through the snow to my office, I passed the wren house. The entry hole was an empty black eye, and I wondered if the wren in question—or any wren—would return. Now he has. It is my understanding that he will prepare two or three nesting sites, then sing about each in hopes of attracting a partner. When I first heard him calling from the cherry tree outside my window, I snuck over for a peek, and there he was, head tipped back and his throat literally bulging with song. I've kept an eye out ever since, and today I can report I've seen him go in and out of the house several times. Unfortunately, I've also seen him calling from a set of low bushes beside the sidewalk, where I already found one dead wren last week. If I knew a little more about wren real estate, I'd help him stage for the showing. Set some earwig-scented candles about the place, throw in some spider egg sacs to help with nest parasites.

Just now he sang again. I went to the window, and he's still popping in and out of the house. It's a pure low-level thrill to watch a bird do exactly what I hoped a bird might do when I hung the little structure last summer. And lest "low-level" sounds derogatory, please note my use of the modifier "pure" and understand that I wrote the line during a stretch when the daily news is positively vibrating with "high-level" thrills, a vibration not dissimilar to that emitted by a 1972 Plymouth Duster just before the left front wheel departs the spindle. You hang a birdhouse, there comes a bird; an infinitesimal fragment of life falls back in place, and the world spins more smoothly.

And then there is that song. Filtered through sun, stillness, and a window screen, as all the best sounds are. The bird jumbles and bumbles and hopes for love, and don't we all.

GOOD-BYE GOLDIE

In a brief ceremony held under cold rain, the loyal hen Goldie, recently removed from the chest freezer where she lay wrapped in a feed bag since her death in winter, was this day buried per my daughter's request beneath a flowering plum tree overlooking the valley.

I had quite forgotten about Goldie until my wife announced that the recent delivery of a batch of venison sausage and weiners (handcrafted by my longtime friend, neighbor, and former firefighting partner Bob the One-Eyed Beagle) had taken up all available freezer space, necessitating that Goldie be removed from where she was tucked between the pork chops and frozen green beans and placed on the garage floor beside the recycling.

Please see to it before the mice or she thaws, said my wife, and fair concerns these.

Goldie was the last bird living from the first flock of chickens we raised the year we moved to this farm, meaning she died at the age of ten. I'm confident she hasn't contributed to an omelet for years. But her pioneer status, soft golden feathers, and gentle demeanor earned her special dispensation long ago. Also, the lobbying of daughters.

It was our younger daughter, arrived on this farm and into this world within weeks of Goldie, who requested the bird be preserved for burial. In most cases we are matter-of-fact about deceased farm animals, but sometimes concession is a no-brainer. Honor, even inconsistently applied, is still honor.

It was the younger, also, who came to my room above the garage today and reminded me that we needed to bury Goldie. I had already forgotten, my head in the perpetual future which on this day included insurance bills.

And so it was out into the rain, across the wet grass of the lawn, and to the spade. First we cut and lifted a neat rectangle of sod. Then we dug past the tree roots. The plum was planted that first year also, in fact atop the placenta after the younger daughter was born upstairs in our farmhouse, proof that being a bachelor for 39 years does nothing to presage life's twists and turns.

We unrolled Goldie's shroud—an empty bag of layer mix —and let her body slip into the grave. There were no tears, and only a smattering of words ("Yep, that's her.") and shortly we were tamping the sod back in place. After a burst of glorious spring it was cold enough that I built a fire this morning, and the child was soon back in front of the wood-stove with her homework while I stowed the shovel and took a photo to commemorate the event. There is the temptation to fish for significance or overdo the poetry, but in this instance I am happy to say that things are as they are, life accretes itself in layers (pun unintended, but I'll take it), and if you're creeped out by the idea of a fully-feathered dead chicken nesting with your frozen broccoli, you should have been around back when my brother John went through his taxidermy phase.

WREN HOUSE PART TWO

The wren house I hung in a chokecherry tree outside my office door last summer is so over-stuffed with sticks bristling out the cracks it appears to have swallowed a porcupine. This is the first any birds have used it. Over the course of the past week, the male—through song and persistence—finally convinced a female to come have a look. It was something to watch him warble her in closer and closer, watch her finally land on the roof, hop back and forth, fly away, return, peek over the eaves to peer into the round portal, then retreat again, over and over, until finally—*pop*—she was in.

By the next day she was fighting to fit twigs thrice her length through the entry. It seemed that four fell to the ground for every one she poked through. By day two her success rate improved. When she grabbed the sticks at one end, rather than in the middle, she did much better. If she got the short end started, the rest of the stick swung backward into parallel with her tail feathers and followed her little body through. If I move close to the window screen I can hear scratching noises as she positions the materials within.

Meanwhile, the male perches in the branches above, warbling madly, narrating his own victories.

Despite all the stick-stuffing, I'm not sure this is a done deal. The pair keep showing up, but they are also gone for long stretches of time, and there is a lot of warbling in the woods and valley all around us. I know the male offers her more than one nesting spot. I'm not sure if the nesting materials mean this is it, or if she's got a backup nest going somewhere else. I don't know if we'll make it to a fuzzy-headed chick poking its head out for a first look at daylight.

I do know it is reassuring to watch birds make a home. There is the implication that the world's cycle is not gone completely a-wobble. But even the standard conditions are risky: Last night when I walked down to put the tractor in the pole barn I found a perfect blue robin's egg on the ground, and this morning a strange black cat was hanging around the yard. When I was checking the chicken water this afternoon, two turkey vultures swung their shadows over the run and the hens scuttled quickly beneath the coop, fearing hawks. Nature gives odds, not insurance.

But that is not what you think of when you step out the door into face-full of perfumed breeze on the first 80-degree day of the year and there are birds singing all around. Around here we learn to love the purifying freeze of subzero air, but at some point you want to be pampered. To bathe in the softer side of backyard nature. Especially when you've had quite enough of human nature.

Birdsong and blossom, dandelions and sun. Chickens easing back out to scratch and peck. A pair of wrens whose eggs may or may not hatch, but proceed as if that is the only outcome.

LUCKY DAY

This morning's fog was nearly as thick in the air as the dew was on the grass. The birds were singing, but their notes were muted in the moisture. Something in the muffled moment implied that a little more time alone and a little less time on the hustle might do the heart good. It also occurred to me that the sensation of being "socked in" on a summer morning is the evocative first cousin to a "snow day," in which all other responsibilities are suspended in the face of Mother Nature.

Lately every time I begin to describe a moment like this I am discomfited by the idea of privilege, a word that in recent times has received renewed consideration and well should. My discomfort grows out of the knowledge that not only do I have very little control over the peace at hand, it has in most respects been handed to me. There are tangible things I can do—and do—to nudge the tipping point toward parity, but I am many lifetimes short of earning what I've been given.

I spent some time this week cleaning out our old granary. There's a scrawl in the concrete over beside the double sliding doors. "1946," it says, and a while back my neighbor Tom said a lot of buildings were built at that time with money and help available for soldiers returning from World War II. I never look at that number without wondering what the conversation might have been the day they poured the concrete. If the crew was short a brother or two, and how the ones who made it back—or didn't have to go in the first place —felt. I've lost track of the times I've looked out the door of that old granary over the valley below and considered the justification of good luck.

Yesterday I phoned a man about some business and smack in the middle of small talk he said his wife had just been diagnosed with cancer. "Just," as in hours ago. She had lived cleanly, done all the right things, and here it was. His voice was a low blend of anger and uncertainty. I had no answers, but I had time. So we talked. And then we took care of business. What else is to be done in the face of imbalance?

I don't have any red-hot answers. Regular trips to the mirror are required. The one with harsh lighting, not the one I worshiped back when I had hair to feather. I'm trying to land somewhere between whiny virtue-signaling and "Hey, neat day!"

Which is where this began. The fog and dew and birds and whatnot. When the chickens were fed I walked out the driveway and back, in part to plan the logistics of the day, but also to be sure this soft morning did not go unnoticed. Soon enough, the sun will burn through.

WEIRD TELEVISION

Once upon a time the world-famous author Neil Gaiman invited me to dinner. He treated me to one of those sushi places where diners sit at a bar facing a miniature river. The rolls and sashimi sail by in teensy boats. You snatch what you want as it bobs past. The boats just keep coming.

Mr. Gaiman was seated to my right. We maintained light conversation. He was sincere in his attention, engaged in his response, and it was a pleasure to share his company. But his gaze conveyed a certain preoccupation. It took me a few minutes, then I pinpointed it: conversation with me was consuming a fraction of his brainpower expressible to the far right of the decimal point, while the rest of his head was fleshing out the plot of the next international blockbuster. Some people hum with intelligence.

We were chatting easily when a woman seated to my left leaned in and hailed Gaiman. She was a tad pushy and I took her for a risible fanatic but it became immediately evident they were familiar, and based on their conversation I deduced they had worked together in Hollywood. Soon I was leaning backward to eat my sushi so they could converse across me. I thanked Neil, excused myself, and returned to my hotel room across the street, where I discovered I had left my television on and tuned to CNBC. The Suze Orman Show was airing, and there, inset on the screen and confessing to Suze she was up to her earlobes in credit card debt with no prospects, was the woman I just left with Neil Gaiman at the sushi bar. I cannot calculate these odds, and assume Neil picked up the tab for her as he did for me.

Then there was the time I was hitchhiking near the Guatemalen border while in pursuit of firefighting stories. I was supplementing my itinerant writer income at the time by writing advertising copy with my friend Al, who as a matter of his own side project landed an infomercial gig, the one in which Al was the guy who encouraged you to order the TIME-LIFE series of "Home Repair and Improvement" books. The commercials were professionally shot with Al standing in a homey kitchen suffused with fake sunlight, and intoning the tagline, "Call now to examine *Decks, Porches and Patios* free for 15 days!" His voice was reverberant velvet.

I was lonely in Central America. Dusty, hungry, and infected with self-pity over a failing relationship, I had been living in hostels and $12 flop rooms, and hitching rides with sugarcane haulers, and so on this day treated myself to a $20 room in the first hotel I found. Trudged upstairs, sat at the end of the bed, and turned on the TV. It glowed slowly to life and then there was my pal Al: "Use your credit card and get this Stanley tape measure *absolutely free!*" I sat there in gap-toothed wonder.

There is no resolution to these anecdotes, other than life is a series of interlinked non sequiturs and possibly time travel. Sometimes events conspire to conspire. Sometimes when you turn on the TV you better be sitting down.

QUOTIDIAN ASPARAGUS

I once wrote of a "most unassuming quotidian hour" and a reader logged in to say I kinda overdid it with "quotidian," and while at first I bristled (I have an ego and have also long maintained we should not let all the fancy people hog all the fancy words), upon a re-read I reckoned she was right on. If that prose wasn't purple it was certainly trending magenta. You hose a rose with enough perfume, you kill it.

But this morning was quotidian in the "ordinary; commonplace" sense of the word, and I'm sticking with it because I needed it. It had been a hectic stretch, graduations and departures and moves and deadlines and the daily headlines, the latter of which evermore resemble pull quotes from a spoof movie that became a hit and you wonder just who's buying all those tickets.

This mawkish (may I?) soup was rendered even more sour when I began the day with a mistake, opening my laptop to work but instead checking those very headlines. Among the dispatches was the news that Anthony Bourdain was dead by his own hand. By now we may know more. It doesn't matter. I just remember reading *Kitchen Confidential* in my old green chair in my old clapboard house in my old hometown, and how it made me want to write, write, write, but how it also made me want to eat. Not just eat fancier (although, to maintain our theme of the day, I don't think we should let fancy people hog all the fancy food, and while I love a deep-fried pickle as much as the next roughneck and the floor of my truck betrays a tendency to buy dinner at gas stations, the idea that you're too country to try capered salmon with asparagus truffle foam is simple reverse snobbery) and take more chances in my own kitchen, but to eat with more range, and above all, appreciation for the food and the world around it. The results were uneven, but they linger.

I read a few of the insta-eulogies, then closed the laptop and wondered if it was permissible to take a nap twenty minutes after getting out of bed. I was rescued from this moral turpitude when I realized I had yet to do the chicken chores. When I opened the hatch they flapped and cackled and hit the grain pans without any apparent appreciation for the finer points of cracked corn versus crumbles. Based on what I've observed upon dumping the table scraps, they'll stab gourmet or gas station with equivalent alacrity.

On the way back through the yard and back to work I stopped to snap several spears of asparagus. The weeds are gaining, and my hands came away wet from reaching through their dew, but as I balanced the shoots in my hand and imagined them rolled in olive oil, peppered, sea-salted, and lightly grilled, that word *quotidian* came to mind and I thought if that is what this hour is, and if for now I am allowed it, I will take it.

WISCO LOOP

Somewhere around Drummond the rain hit as if slung from great sopping towels. A descendent wind pushed the roadside trees into looping swipes and for a mile or so it seemed possible they would scrub the car. The National Weather Service broke into the radio broadcast with a flash flood warning. A mile later the rain was a light spatter, and then it was done. By the time I reached my destination just south of Bayfield the air was humid and still, with here and there a seam of sun through the overcast.

The following day I drove Highway 2 along Chequamegon Bay through Ashland (with a quick stop at the Black Cat Coffeehouse, of which I have long been a fan due to its creaky wooden floors, faint whiff of patchouli, and reliably stout coffee), traversed the Bad River Reservation, and eventually dropped south on Highway 51 down to Plover. I have nothing profound to report beyond the fact that even after 53 years of residency I am still caught off guard at the depth and profusion of green this state can bud up by early June.

There is a temptation on my part—due in part to

Kerouac's *On The Road*, Steinbeck's *Travels With Charley*, and a whole lotta truckin' songs—to offer up some significant take on the state of things based on what I see through the windshield, overhear at the gas station, or infer from the tailgater who just ached to pass me for five miles up there above Woodruff and finally blew by just in time to hit the 30 mile an hour zone, but in fact sometimes on these drives the cogitation is mundane. I spun around the AM radio dial (actually turning the knob click-by-click so as not to get cheated out of some faint, static-wrapped preaching or ranting or 401k advice), I thought about my children in terms of what effect my absences might have, I stopped and called my mom, I bought a butter burger under the pretext of using the restroom, whenever I passed one of the few remaining one-story motels I tried to imagine the lot filled with big boaty Fords and Buicks towing wooden watercraft, I wondered if anyone's mind had ever been changed by a bumper sticker, I noticed the dead deer had antlers in velvet, and—just as I passed Stevens Point—wondered if I could justify another butter burger.

Tomorrow, if weather and the world and our old van allow (I have high hopes, as the gas tank was recently reattached to the chassis with fresh straps), I will head west on Highway 10 and make my way back to our little country home, completing a loop of just over 500 miles. As always happens after these excursions, my mind will stay in motion after my body stops. Like hubcap spinners rotating at a stoplight, the sensation of a road trip lingers, even as we stare at the hearth. It is good to be home. It is good to be free. And let others be.

NORTHERN MEMORIAL

My longtime friend and bandmate Billy and I drove seven hours round trip to Bayfield and back for a memorial service yesterday. Billy had to return that same evening because he was to sing at another memorial service the following morning, which is to say he has reached that age (and I am rapidly sliding into it) at which memorial services begin to compete for room on the calendar with medical appointments, prescription refills, and a diminishing number of contemporary birthdays.

I call Billy my longtime friend and he is, but we met fairly late in our lives, me into my 30s, him into his more-than-thats. He was a seasoned performer, I was a guy who had only just learned three chords, then one day we looked up and we were into our second decade of sharing a stage. There are many ways to quantify friendship, but I'd suggest that the ability to converse nonstop over the course of seven hours even though you already know all of each other's stories ranks right up there. The greatest hits are still knee-slappers.

Billy is just far enough ahead of me in the game of life

that he is an invaluable mentor when it comes to advice on anything from hot mustard to harmonies on the bridge, but in no area has he helped me more than in my roles as parent and husband. Without being intrusive or bossy, he has a powerful ability to get me to take stock of my performance in both settings. We were eastbound on Highway 2 when he said something about how to judge a man by how he helps with the boxes on moving day and by 11 p.m. that very evening I was quoting him word-for-word to my 18 year-old daughter as we shared leftover takeout in the kitchen after she got home from work. And if my wife notices I don't default to certain ingrained bad habits quite so quickly for a week or so, she has Billy to thank.

The man we memorialized was the husband of another friend and bandmate. Late in life these two folks found in each other the kind of match we all hope for, only to have it cut terribly short by illness. Billy and I talked about memorials and the power inherent of the physical presence of friends in times of grief and honor, and how for all the mundane cruelty and foolishness afoot in the world, we crave these little shavings of peace and decency carved from the hardness.

There percolates in Billy the seeds of a terminal illness that is currently held at bay. Lately the numbers have bumped a touch. But here's another thing about Billy: He spent his life building, setting, and updating gravestones. No matter where we drive together, he's always pointing up this shady road or over that rise, naming a cemetery tucked into the landscape. You'd be hard-pressed to find a one in which he has not knelt to engrave a date to the right of the dash. The job imbued him with matter-of-fact sense of mortality. We talk about this a lot, the idea that neither of us takes one single second for granted. "This won't be the last memorial you and I will attend together," Billy said at one point during our trip. "Yah, one more at the very least," I said. When he got the implication, he guffawed without reservation, and this is why I cherish him so.

WREN HATCH

The first time the wrens shacked up outside my office window, the deal fell through. The male chittered, burbled, and coaxed, and eventually the female stuffed the miniature house with sticks, but then both birds quite literally flew the coop. Things were quiet for a few weeks. I suspect they raised a brood elsewhere. Then they (or wrens who looked very like them) returned. The male ran through his repertoire, the female delivered a few more sticks, and then over the course of the past three weeks they've been steadily present.

Meanwhile the world has festered along. I recently asked a question in public, question being, "How loud you gotta pray to drown out all the contradictions?" I wasn't really taking a poll, but folks certainly responded. "Not sure, but unceasingly," was my favorite reply.

These days asking questions in public is like pulling the toilet handle while standing in the bowl. You long for discourse of the sort extolled by the currently dead French philosopher Montaigne, who wrote, "Harmony is a wholly tedious quality in conversation," which at first sounds exactly like what we've got, until you consider he didn't stick the word *conversation* in there by accident. He predicated that line on the idea that even in disagreement we'd actually talk to each other, not over or through each other, not via the digital shroud of an avatar, and he certainly didn't expect that we'd settle for pelting our next-door neighbors with secondhand epithets spewed from a rich distance by folks the Irish poet Seamus Heaney once perfectly classified as "mouth athletes."

But here we are. And, of course, Montaigne knew the world wasn't wired for compatibility, writing as he was during a time when his neighbors were killing and torturing each other by the thousands over religion and royalty and a mishmash of both. He knew his largest responsibility was to maintain his own character. I try to remember that daily, and fail just as often. When it comes to choosing sides, my previously declared criteria remain: How you treating my family? How you treating my neighbors? Everything else is just hatchets and meringue.

But what am I saying here that's original, or doesn't make me sound like a whiny old man? Or worse, a whiny, *preachy* old man. My chief daily task presents itself in my bathroom mirror every day at dawn. This morning I didn't linger. Did the chicken chores, and headed to work. The path to my office passes beneath the chokecherry tree where the wren house is hung. The hole the birds pass through is at ear level, and for the first time, I heard teensy cheeping within. An hour later I looked out the window just in time to see one of the adults enter with an inchworm in its beak. The wrens are doing their work, I must do mine.

SUNDAY NIGHT SADS

The light was fading as we left the home farm up north. My wife was away at a wedding and the elder daughter had other commitments, so it was just the younger child and me in the van. The countryside was soft green, and right after the first turn we stopped to watch a yearling deer standing shin-deep in ditchwater. The deer was unafraid of the van, but twitched its ears when we rolled down the window and whistled at it.

We moved on to Turkey Corners, where I flipped the headlights on but it was not yet dark enough for them to reflect from the stop sign. When we crossed the big swamp the floodlights of the sand plant were visible on the horizon and the sun was well sunk but the sky was still dim blue. As we approached the edge of the tiny town where I attended kindergarten through graduation, an Amish buggy met us at the intersection. Its headlights and turn signals shone in contrast to the boxy blackness of the rig. By the time we passed the village's single glowing gas station and hit the four-lane the gloaming was fully upon us.

The gloaming is a tricky time, especially when Mom is gone. Just as I set the cruise control my young one announced that she had "the Sunday night sads." Looking out over the darkening landscape, I understood. I am susceptible myself. The gradual emergence of distant yard lights as the last drop of rose leaves the sky only exacerbates the issue.

I drew the child's attention to a light flashing in the sky off to the southeast. "I think that's the flight from Chicago," I said. It often passes over our farm on approach, although by this point it had already made its wide turn. I was pointing out the plane as a way of buying myself time, since I possess no real antidote to the Sunday night sads. I was hoping that we might pass under the plane just as it made its final approach, as even in this advanced gadgeted age, there is still something cool about a big plane flying right overhead. Unfortunately it was on a different vector and the lights descended out of sight long before we were anywhere near.

We passed through the city shortly, a cacophony of lights, visible from our farm as a gauzy inverted bowl, and by the time we dipped to our home valley I was studying all the reflective elements of the guard rail and general directional signs, even out here on the back roads, and wondering what it was to drive this country back before safety ruled all, and then I realized the drive home had evolved into a meditation on the emotional power of light.

After tucking the car into the garage, I sent the young one in to brush her teeth and go to bed, promising I would be in shortly to tuck her in and kiss her goodnight. Then I walked down to close up the chicken coop. A lone firefly winked and disappeared, a remnant straggler from the glowing thousands plying the valley just weeks ago, and no match for the emergent constellations above. I shut off the kitchen light and climbed the stairs in the dark, then sat on the edge of the bed to tell the little girl we loved her, that the Big Dipper was still solid in the sky, and that there would be sunshine in the morning.

ROUGHNECK REVELATIONS

A long time ago backstage at a state fair in Petaluma, California, a country music roadie told me, "If you see food, eat it; if you got ten minutes, sleep." The concision and clarity of that advice is capable of vaporizing a decade's worth of self-help books. It is a phrase tattooed upon my soul if not my skin, and just last weekend I deployed it on a young stagehand acting tentative in the presence of free scrambled eggs.

I remember also a rainstorm that struck while I was running forklift for a local sawyer famed as much for his bar fights as his straight 2x4s. He was built like walk-in beer cooler and was known to polka with women balanced upon his beef-quarter shoulders. I was a churchly teen who had yet to kiss a girl, let alone sport one bodily about a tavern, and so I suspect it was as much overcompensation as work ethic that drove me to continue running racks of lumber even as the rain hammered down and the rest of the crew ran for the shelter of a beat-up van. Shortly the side door cracked, the sawyer's head emerged, and he bellowed, "HEY! Even a *chicken* has enough sense to get in out of the rain!" Thus encouraged, I bailed off the forklift to join them inside the muscle-packed van thick with the scent of sweat and wet and sawdust and bar oil, the rain ringing off the roof like tympani.

And then there was the ranch boss in Wyoming, who, upon overhearing me confiding to another ranch hand that I was entertaining overtures from a young woman who had at that time accumulated a reputation for escapades far exceeding my ability to keep up, let alone reciprocate, fixed me with a steady gaze and said, "Son, run like you was bein' shot at!" Naturally, I ignored him, which I do not regret, because how else might I have learned for certain that he was right on?

It was from this man's father—the original ranch boss— that I first heard the phrase, "A fish factory stinks after three days." Later I would discover the words were not original with him, but every time I hear them they evoke an image of him standing on the hot gravel driveway of the ranch yard, the dust from the wheels of the dismissed character in question still hanging in the air. Trust your instincts, I learned, and in cases of uncertainty, give it three days.

When I directed the young stagehand to eat them eggs and grab a nap last Saturday, I felt seasoned and wise. Later he will learn what I have learned, that we cannot live by aphorism alone, that context and complication will have their say, that time reshapes us all. Specifically I was dozily eyeing the free doughnuts beside the free eggs while absently pinching my gut just above the beltline, and considering exactly when "If you see food, eat it; if you got ten minutes, sleep," transformed from my credo to my default.

GARLIC IN

The garlic is drying on the racks. This is bittersweet news, as the ceremony of the pulling of the garlic is one of the first moments of summer when you admit summer isn't getting any younger. But it is sweet to know that the bulbs we stuffed into their dirt pillow last fall wintered well and come spring thaw performed their mitotic magic, transforming a single clove into the clusters we tugged from the earth today.

As with many of the more stable elements of my life, the garlic is a testament to my wife. It was she who first suggested we plant it, and she who made sure we actually followed through, and now we are entering our second decade of homegrown. In fact, during those years when circumstances precluded us having a full garden, the garlic beds have never lain fallow.

My younger daughter would like you to know that her father's phrase "the ceremony of the pulling of the garlic" is as usual wishfully poetic and does not reflect her perception of the experience, especially at the beginning, when there was a brief period of negotiation regarding the terms of the day. Continuing under the category of wishfully poetic, she would like you to know that the term "negotiation" in this case is being willfully misused as she was allowed to state her terms but was then overruled not by vote but by dictate, as the adults in her home continue to insist they are in charge.

The elder daughter was off at work, and my wife off to an out-of-state family wedding, so it was just we two. Under open skies and the rhythm of the work her mood soon mellowed, and shortly the chore was being narrated via the voices of assorted characters made up as we went along. This narration continued even as we drove the truckload of pulled garlic down to the pole barn, where we distributed it across the drying racks. Here my daughter would again draw your attention to Dad's propensity for poesy, as what we are talking about here is a bunch of misshapen wire panels from the old chicken yard laid flat over a wagon rack featuring one flat tire. This "temporary" garlic-drying solution has been in place now for over five years.

There was an interesting moment a few seasons ago when a sheriff's deputy, canvassing our buildings for a fugitive, discovered the drying racks. Boy, he homed right in on them. I was able to pretty quickly prove my case using the bulbs as exculpatory evidence, but the look in his eyes when first he espied the operation betrayed the fact that he was not thinking first and foremost about gastronomy.

Now we wait as the sun—with the steel pole barn serving as a giant kiln—draws the moisture from the stems and blades while concentrating the cloves. We will hardly have begun consuming them by the time we steal a small boxful, break them apart, and stick them in the same earth, yet another gesture of hope for things basic, and things poetic.

APPROPO MALAPROPS

Last Sunday a bunch of us were up at the home farm shooting the breeze in lawn chairs around the fire pit when my father got to telling the one about old RJ up the road who owned a tiny patch of pine trees situated in one corner of a forty-acre square. The remainder of the forty had been bought up by a big-time crop farmer. At one point the big-time farmer installed a circle irrigator, but he was frustrated by RJ's pine trees, as they blocked the irrigator from describing a complete orbit. Negotiations ensued, terms were arranged, and in the end RJ sold his pine tree patch for—as he told my father—an "exuberant" price. The smile on RJ's face was such that Dad has never been quite sure if he chose "exuberant" over "exorbitant" on purpose, but in any case he made the better choice.

This led to a discussion of what I call "appropo mala-props," in which the wrong word is in fact the far better word. In this our cloud-based age, curated lists of examples are a clickety-tap away, but as we were sitting in a relaxed circle on a country evening while the family children played on swings, we didn't want to risk diving into the hand-held

looking glass with all its mephitic distractions, and instead
began rattling off our favorites by memory. One involved two
volunteer firefighters engaging in an extramarital situation.
When they used the local fire hall for an assignation and
someone found out, the small-town fire chief claimed this,
"just exasperated the situation," and he was not wrong.

Children are a font of words beautifully misused,
including the child who, hoisting a satchel of fruit, told me,
"This bag is plump full!" and another, watching a bus pull
away from the curb of a human-jammed airport terminal
with a load of weary rental car customers aboard, informed
me, "That's an airport shuffle." She was right on and would
agree with me that half the people on that bus were suffering
what an overtired emailer once spelled as "sleep deprava-
tion," just one letter off and all the better for it.

That last example reminds me that not all appropo mala-
props are funny, nor are they spoken—some are the result of
typos and can be downright poetic. I am thinking here of the
time I read a manuscript in which the following beautiful
error slipped through: "The land, which is toiled by a local
farmer..." If only I could make mistakes of that quality on a
regular basis.

I once received an email from someone explaining there
would be a delay in a project because one of the main players
was "in the final throngs of divorce." So sad, so true, and I
assume some of the throng were billing by the hour.

Finally, there was the speaking event where a woman
placed one of my books on the table before me, opened it to
the title page, and said, "Can you sign this for a friend of
mine? She's an expiring writer."

I scribbled as fast as I could.

FIRST HEARSE DATE

The fact that I was unmarried until my 39th year may be traceable to the fact that when Lisa Kettering invited me to the Sadie Hawkins dance I picked her up in a hearse driven by my friend Bob who went by the name Bullwinkle.

This was my first date. Ever. I was not sure how these things went. As I recall we sat three abreast in the front seat, despite all the room available in the back. Shoulder to shoulder we arrived at the high school gymnasium. I recall there were straw bales, and further adding to the glory of the evening for Lisa I warned her beforehand that due to personal religious strictures I was not allowed to actually dance at the Sadie Hawkins dance. We may have snuck a near-motionless slow one, but mostly I just remember sitting there while Lisa talked to the other girls. When Bullwinkle and I dropped her off that night I saw her safely to her door but there was no kiss as I was both too dumb and too dumbstruck to know what to do other than say goodnight. I don't believe I tried to shake her hand, but my memory is fogged by time and obstructed by cringing.

The subject of Bullwinkle's hearse surfaced at my class

reunion last week. Despite the vivid nature of the preceding anecdote, I hadn't thought of the vehicle in years. It turns out several of my classmates had their own stories about it. For the sanctity of friendship and school pride I choose to share just one, which I find extra delightful in that thirty-five years after the fact, this was the first I heard it told: Two of my classmates—we'll call them Snake and Harley—used to don evening wear then run up Chetek way with Bullwinkle and the hearse and a bunch of loosely assembled boards meant to resemble a coffin. Upon approaching the city limits, Harley would exit the hearse, recline supine on the shoulder of the road, and arrange the lumber loosely around himself. Meanwhile, Snake and Bullwinkle would continue into town, pull a U-turn, and wait for traffic. When a car appeared, Bullwinkle would accelerate to where Harley lay tangled in the remnants of his fake coffin, brake abruptly, and swerve to a stop beside the road, at which point he and Snake—impeccably attired—would bail out, sprint to the back of the hearse, open the gate, gather up Harley's limp body, throw him inside, chuck the coffin lumber in after him, then slam the gate, tromp the gas, and accelerate out of sight.

Bullwinkle was the first of our class to die. His was not an easy life. Giggles and sweet remembrances mitigate none of this. I have no idea where Lisa Kettering wound up. Montana, I heard, but that was many reunions ago. Snake, though, Snake is alive and well and was there at the tavern to tell the tale, and he told it well. The hearse is coming, but today we travel laughing.

WILDLIFE CENSUS

This morning when I stepped outside I spooked a buck in velvet. This would speak to our rural existence were the suburbs not thick with whitetails. Same with the coyotes, which seem to have taken a downturn this year. I still hear them, but the rabbit population is on the rise again, a sign that the balance of nature is shifting. Perhaps the coyotes are all over by the mall, hunting discarded French fries and redeeming Star Rewards at the drive-through.

The owls are as thick as ever, their calls booming the woods nightly. Yesterday around midnight when I was leaving the office several of them got into a screeching match the likes of which I've never heard. What started out as a standard cross-valley "Who cooks for you?" exchange suddenly blew up in my back yard when what sounded like three different owls flew in to land directly overhead in a maple grove. I couldn't see them, but the sound was immediate and startling. The standard hooting was replaced by what sounded like a gathering of drunken roosters and crying babies. I couldn't see the birds, but it was a raucous squall.

I've seen no fishers this year. They're furtive, and I've had only two sightings in the eleven years we've lived here. In both cases the animal was crossing our driveway. A fisher is a weasel on a lift kit and steroids, and a central reason we lock the chicken coop door every night. Plus, we do have your standard weasels.

Bears, the same as fishers; haven't seen any, but I know they're around. Now and then I spy a paw print in the mud, and I frequently find corn or grass wallered and squashed in a pattern consistent with bruin behavior. Also, the land was loaded with berries this summer, so the buffet was set. Of all the animals common around these parts, I marvel most at how rare it is to see a bear outside of a hunting situation, big and black as they are.

It's been a while since I've seen any indication of wolves, but we had at least one around here a couple of years back. I discovered a number of kill scenes, and once when I was up writing at 3 a.m., a wolf howled behind the pole barn, a sound you don't soon forget and tends to drop the temperature of your spine.

We are all set on moles and ground squirrels.

This random census as provided is a celebration of bucolic living, but it is also a reflection of my shortcomings, specifically that despite my status as a ruralist I am no naturalist and not even a generalist but a superficialist, living in and amongst the animals, noting them and appreciating them (whenever I see velvet antlers in the wild I get a thrill akin to spotting a working class unicorn) but hardly able to tell you what those owls were up to, or break down the whole stoat/weasel/ermine thing. In short, I am no Mark Trail. At best I am Mike Back Forty, and my invocation of Mark Trail speaks to an entirely different issue of demographics and possibly gerontology.

NORTH SHORE

We are returning from an inspection tour of Lake Superior's North Shore, specifically the region between Duluth and Grand Marais. I can report that it is good to stare at holes carved in rock by water as a way of reminding myself that despite the dumb damage we do, human behavior is irrelevant, long-term cosmos-wise. This is a problematic statement and open to parsing. Talk amongst yourselves.

This was a quick trip, and quickly planned. It was also bittersweet in that it was potentially the final family jaunt comprised of our long-term four-person configuration. There is plenty of reason to think that our recent high school graduate will join us on future trips, but she is working two jobs and reading maps, there is college in the offing, and changes —planned and unplanned—will come.

For now though, we packed the car and hit the road as our standard familial foursome. We marveled at the giant silos lining the ports, we speculated on the contents of the ships, we wondered why there were so many dead birch trees (a sign at an interpretive center suggested it might be from deer eating the smaller birch, it has been going on for some time, and conservation efforts are underway), we ate home-made sandwiches from a cooler, and Dad may have lobbied to detour for non-homemade coffee. We made some roadside stops and brief forays to view waterfalls and walk the lakeshore, and over the course of two days completed a number of light hikes. In the evenings we made and ate dinner together, laughed, and told old stories. It was by defin-ition, as the hack phrase has it, "quality family time." For purposes of keeping it real, I should add there was also grumping and sniping, and certain impromptu hiking pep talks were required. The foundations of family are bound to crack; the best mortar is elastic.

Rather than list our favorite stops in the manner of a trav-elogue, I just hope you get your own chance to poke around up there. Among the many pet peeves I should eradicate and/or keep to myself is my tendency to get bucky when someone hears I'm going on a trip and says, "Oh you *have* to stop at x, y, or z!" Nope, I don't *have* to do anything, in fact that's why I'm going on this trip. So if you head up along Minnesota's North Shore, you do what you want. You can't really mess it up. I am glad we hiked up to Devil's Kettle Falls but even more glad I had never seen photos of it in advance, because having lowered my expectations (we had a "Devil's Teacup" in the woods a few miles from our home farm, and while it was unusually deep and round, it was in the end just a real deep dry hole and fun for sledding) I was not prepared for the dramatic sight and mystery of it. This concludes my travel tips.

PERPETUAL PORTRAIT

As common as deer snorts are around these parts I didn't find the sharp exhalations out of the ordinary at first, but when they continued one after the other I left the writing desk to peek out the window and see what all the fuss was for. It was midafternoon and sunny and the cat was hurrying up the driveway. Not running, but hurrying and looking back over its shoulder. Odd behavior for a cat. And then, busting out of the brush, a buck deer, trotting behind and shaking its velvety antlers at the fleeing feline. As they chased past the window I grabbed my phone, hoping for some sort of viral social media renown, but by the time I got to video mode the cat was in deep cover beneath kitchen window hedge and the buck—with a final stamp and snort—was off into the woods behind the pole barn, so you'll just have to take my word for it.

As any cave drawing will establish, the compulsive need to document everything and share it with the world is by no means a recent phenomenon, but technology has certainly kicked it into overdrive. I've dabbled myself, sometimes justifying it as a way to help me make a living, other times just because I want to publicly declare, "Hey. Look at this weird mushroom."

This past Sunday morning we gathered at my mother-in-law's house for family portraits. All things considered, I prefer dentist appointments, but know when it is my job to show up, shut up, and smile. It was the usual multi-generational rodeo. Lots of contradictory commands, exhortations, and inevitable tears, but our faces have been recorded for history and some of us will appear happy to be there.

Later that afternoon the extended family gathered in the basement to watch a digital slide show of past gatherings. First we had to pause a children's movie in progress. There were protestations, but the second the first slide flashed on the big flat screen the happiest cries came from the youngest among us. Photo by photo, memory by memory, we adults murmured and chuckled and nudged each other, but the toddler set was positively giddy, pointing with delight at photos of themselves on a pontoon boat, or around a campfire, or whacking a piñata, or just eating potato salad.

"I looked so different then!" exclaimed my five-year-old nephew when he saw a photo of himself as a four-year-old, and in that moment it occurred to me that the power of the viral video in the blow-up moment pales in comparison to the power of the standard family snapshot in retrospect. The wonder in that child's voice was real, and the shelf-life of that snapshot will invest it with greater power the older it gets. Once you've seen a deer chasing a cat it will never surprise you again, whereas the joy of seeing yourself happy among family will only refresh itself in rediscovery. I still wish I had captured the deer harassing the cat. The kids would have loved it. But they have a thousand other pictures. A thousand other joys, viral across generations.

NANETTE

Each year I am happily surprised by the pulsing galaxy of fireflies strung throughout our yard and seaming the valley below and also regularly moved to write it up in some form or another. That is all well and good and artistically obvious, but what about the bug that blinked at me just last week, so far behind the original flash mob I was surprised all over again? The outlier: there's your story.

It was the usual setting: I was crossing the yard come nighttime to secure the chicken coop. I enjoy the martial import of the verb "secure" but in fact it's just me stumbling over mole hills in the dark while wearing rubber sandals (can't name them until the endorsement deal is finalized) (negotiations ongoing and completely one-sided in that the other party is uninvolved and unaware) at the end of a day that was—if standard standards were met—likely 10% progress, 20% failure, 15% lost to general waffling, 50% put off 'til tomorrow, and the remainder scrubbed from memory. More often than not, dropping the tiny door that keeps the chickens weasel-free is the most decisive move I make all day.

In other words, it is unlikely I was in a reflective or ruminative state of mind when the solo insect flickered yellow-green from the weeds alongside the pole barn, and perhaps it was thus all the more surprising; all the more bracing. It is possible—in the mind-fog of all the things left unfinished at close of day, of the health insurance premium due, of not wishing to catch a toe and face-plant among the burdock, of early June having become late August—I had forgotten that they even existed. It happens.

What is it like to be a firefly late to the firefly parade? Surely it diminishes your opportunities for love. How dark it must seem, just you weakly winking with nothing but the cold universe of stars as witness and them ice blue and staring, no rhythm at all. On the upside, you stand out from the crowd, the crowd having gone dark. There is also the distinction (before your extinction) of delivering the final blink of the year. You are the last to flash. It is your light that will linger in the mind of those least expecting you.

But: The outlier life is rarely easy. Last night my wife and I viewed comedian Hannah Gadsby's show "Nanette," which, if you've watched it, you know takes a turn midway through, shifting from humor to...well, you'll need to see for yourself. It ain't comfortable, I'll tell you that. Nor is it intended to be, nor should it be. In retrospect I can draw parallels to the lightning bug arc. At first, a flurry of chuckles. Then a thinning out. And then nothing funny at all. Just darkness. And then, at the end—in Gadsby's refusal to give into anger although given every right—a concluding flash of hope. Of love. Even as she refuses to let me off the hook. Even as the light of the last firefly cannot warm away the coming winter.

The common denominator here lies in the power of the outlier speaking out. Streaming a comedy special in search of a laugh, I was drawn to examine my conscience. Crossing the yard expecting nothing but darkness, I saw light.

MEMORY HOLE

Today I spent several hours going through old videotapes of me wandering around my hometown and local countryside telling stories. There were entertaining moments (I had forgotten the sideburns!), wistful moments (shots of my old pickup truck back before the rear axle froze up) confusing moments (whatever happened to that green parka, the one that could have doubled as a car cover and smelled of mice, rubber, and the 1970s?), bewildering moments (entire stretches of dialogue—conceived, written, and delivered by me—of which I had no memory at all), and a multitude of moments that were simply fun to revisit.

But when the last clip went to black, I found myself ruminating on how we hold the past, as opposed as to how we hold *on* to the past.

I've been running this Mobius mind-groove for a while now, but it kicked up a gear when I turned 50. It's a soupy thought-conundrum based on mulling a desire to simultaneously honor the past, build on the past while navigating the present, and remain open to—shoot, to even *welcome*—the future. I admit we are in freshman dorm territory here, only

AARP-legal and without the weed, but I'm too deep in the stew to stop now. Hopefully next week it'll be back to zippy anecdotes about chickens.

The thing is, I have watched so many of my elders grow fearful and brittle with time. I am distinguishing here between standing on principle and simply standing in the way. In some of those old videos I was joking about how things are "around here." I was nodding in my heart when my head suggested things weren't that way at all anymore, and in some cases maybe never shoulda been that way in the first place.

I am being deliberately vague, as I don't want to send anyone down a specific rabbit hole. Life has enough hounds howling in the comment threads. I'm just trying to call my own memories into question. Not to dismiss them. Not to cease enjoying them. But to see them the way someone else might have seen them. And perhaps gently break it to my memories that I am grateful for the time they gave me but we are moving into a new phase now.

I am not surrendering reminiscence. I'm just not gonna wear it around like a forty-pound vulcanized parka (which is probably in a box in a shed). I'm going to work to see the future through the eyes of those younger than I. Hear it in the words of those who speak differently than I. Discover it via the minds of those who conceive of a world that includes me but need not center on me.

In this the age of binaries and snark, the preceding paragraphs have set me up to come off as half-baked, mealy-mouthed, and short on details. So be it. Sometimes the only way to learn something is to say something and then just sit there and take whatever ricochets. Sometimes the only way to move the world forward is to get out of the way. Whatever the case, it is long past time to get rid of that parka.

BUTTERFLY CHICKENS

Last week after a run of heavier postings I promised I'd write something about chickens. Now they are right across the yard there, holding me to it. I would like to think I am in their good graces, having just two days ago put them on fresh grass, including some rapeseed plants sprung up between the thistle and foxtail. I sowed the rapeseed this spring with all good intentions only to see the quack and pigweed blow up and smother it. Mid-summer I brush-hogged the whole bunch, so the resurgent succulents are a sweet late-season surprise. The chickens have already pecked them down to spines.

I've also been tossing windfall apples into the run, a tricky proposal this time of year as most of the fruit—especially the apples gnawed by deer—is infested with worker wasps. The "worker" element of their job description completed for the season and with nothing on the to-do list but die, the wasps spend their last sunshiny days in sucking cider from the source. This is called making the best of a bad situation. It looks like B-roll for a death metal video. You don't want a handful of it.

So: For the fowl, fresh peckings. But if you wait for gratitude from a chicken you will wait a while, and this morning it was nothing but the usual flap and hustle when I loosed them from the coop. They bailed straight for the feed buckets with nary a nod. One of the roosters crowed and tried to hustle a hen who simply wanted breakfast, a rolling exhibition of the usual male inanities wrapped in feathers.

We've discussed dispensing with the poultry. We've kept a flock from the first spring we moved to this old farm and we treasure the eggs, but lately there has been some generational gear-shifting and talk of spending time in other places, and although it is now possible to raise and lower a chicken door via the web and our neighbor Denny is ever graciously available, animal husbandry was never intended to be conducted by remote even if alls you got is a few raggedy birds. Lots of times lately life would just run more smoothly without them. We'll see.

Down there past the coop I ran the brush-hog wide around a couple of big milkweed patches, left them to stand. We've done that all around the place, and this summer there were monarch butterflies everywhere. Somewhere the earth is keeping score and certainly our milkweed will not be enough to win the game but I'd like to think we're at the very least making up for those I've killed with my minivan, hello culpability on wheels. The world is complex. Not so the mind of a chicken. For now we'll keep them, if only for the tether they provide to a universe in need of more eggs and more butterflies. Tomorrow I will again move them to fresh pasture, possibly let them in among the milkweed now that the Monarchs have flown.

STORM SONG

The wind arrived with a freight train sound, advanced by a wall of hot, pudding-thick air. I was off for town to retrieve the young one from play rehearsal, and paused at the base of the hill to check my phone for storm warnings. Tornado watch, it said, and just then the rain hit with a thousand fat smacks, like the van roof was being machine-gunned with spitwads. A mile down the road I was traveling ten miles an hour and the van was rocking in the wind.

Another mile and the winds lifted and the rain thinned. By the time I pulled up in front of the theater, the precipitation had settled to a soft wash.

Around here, "town" is creeping ever closer. It's disorienting to be in the chicken coop or woodshed and then ten minutes later cruise past the Starbucks. On the upside, if you've got a kid who likes to do plays, you can work the logistics while still providing her precious counterbalancing opportunities to stack firewood, run a pitchfork, and clean out nesting boxes. I am a far-end of the dead-end road sort of fellow by raising and inclination but have been treated very well by city people over the years, so I am taking a wait-and-see attitude on the encroaching development. I prefer the back forty but should I wind up living the downtown life, there are worse things than waking within walking distance of groceries and cappuccinos. And I wouldn't miss the yearly Attaching of the Snowplow, otherwise known as the Ceremony of Irrational Anger Directed Toward Inanimate Objects.

I enjoy the trips to and from rehearsal as they mean the child is trapped in the car with me for 15-20 minutes depending on the stoplights, and based on my accumulated parenting experience thus far there is nothing like a moving vehicle to corral a child into talking to you. When my elder daughter was a teen but still too young to drive, she always knew when she climbed into the front seat for a ride home from volleyball practice, there was a 50/50 shot the old man would be in sermon mode at some point, all the while maintaining a speed that made it impractical to bail out and still be able to play volleyball.

Indeed, on the trip home post-storm, I did bring the younger child up to speed on some evolving "expectations," but for most of the ride we sang along to silly old songs on the radio and remarked on the evidence of the storm strewn across the roadway. As we made the final turn I had to brake and then squeeze through the space between a large fallen tree and the guardrail. It wasn't until later, when I was in bed and drifting off to sleep, that I realized that based on the timing of the initial downburst that tree would have fallen within 30 seconds of my driving through that very space. Storms are always coming, and so much is up to chance; all the more reason to raise our voices in song, silly or sacred.

MONTAIGNE AND MERCY

I have been lately revisiting my old friend Michel de Montaigne. In fact I rarely stop pestering him. It's a figurative and lopsided relationship what with him having died in 1592. His *Essais* have long been a favorite read and re-read of mine, but just recently I've been chewing my way through a book called *Montaigne and the Quality of Mercy*. I got the tome by chance and charity while I was passing through Viroqua, Wisconsin, where Eddy Nix of Driftless Books opened the door to his bibliophilic barn and said, "Go ahead, take one." This is a questionable business model, and I went for it, heading directly for the philosophy shelves. I spotted Montaigne's name on a spine, and searched no further.

Montaigne and the Quality of Mercy was published 20 years ago. Author David Quint is a professor of English and comparative literature at Yale. I hope he doesn't mind me reading his work while plopped in a tree stand, because it is getting to be that time of year. His wouldn't be the first of my books to smell faintly of Tink's #69. That last is what you call a niche reference; those of you who need to get it will.

But: *mercy.* It seems quixotically quaint to give this

concept quiet consideration while the national conversation "unfolds" like a wasp-infested slime typhoon, but in the preface, Quint reminds me that Montaigne was living and writing in a time of civil war. He observed firsthand, Quint writes, the damage done by "the hard-liner who never yields," whose "obstinate virtue" has boiled down to pride and self-interest. Instead, Montaigne was interested in a "pliant goodness" that might result in a spirit of accommodation manifest as mercy.

That's all from just the first page of the preface. I've already made a lot of underlines, and have read some paragraphs six or eight times. It's an escape of sorts, this kind of reading. Human thought and behavior set in ink, pinned to the page so it can be studied and re-studied as opposed to the non-stop online outrage scrolling to which I am commonly susceptible. The static page encourages rationality. And reflection.

When I settle in with a book like *Montaigne and the Quality of Mercy*, I am reading above my pay grade. There is stuff here I couldn't parse if you gave me chopsticks and a forklift. But I love the cotton-headed tussle of it. And the *access* of it: The idea that I might take the better products of Yale ("better" inserted with specific intent) up a tree stand purchased at Menards and emerge from the woods more broad-minded; more merciful. I still gotta do the chicken chores and pay the electric bill and empty the dehumidifier and I'm not in line for sainthood or tenure or a position of paid punditry, and I still like eating Slim Jims, gas station doughnuts, the Packers, and wow there's still a lot of pages to go, but the last phrase I underlined before placing the book flat for now was, "some form of human dignity is indispensible," and that'll do to pursue for now.

DUMP RAKE HALLOWEEN

Denny and Linda, our neighbors down the hill, have put out their Halloween display. The whole thing is built around an old dump rake. "Old" in this instance is redundant, as dump rakes have been out of common use for generations now (new ones are available but they're either for your lawn or giant versions designed for large-scale haymaking operations) and in fact, even I, having first raked hay over 40 years ago, remember ours only as a monument; unused, tucked back in the pines, wrapped in weeds and booby-trapped with blackberry canes. It had been parked there by the previous owner of the farm and we never used it. I remember sitting on the steel-dish seat, pulling at the levers and pushing at the pedal, unsure how any of it worked, but imagining I was rolling up long windrows of thick timothy, the comb-curved tines sticking out behind like a bustle. Other times the dump rake was a spaceship. Or a steam-powered paddleboat. Like most abandoned farm implements of the time it was originally horse-drawn, but the shaft had been updated to accept a tractor tongue and hitch pin. Still, I never saw it move until the day Dad sent it to the scrapyard.

So the first thing that happens when I see Denny and Linda's setup is I get a nice little bump of nostalgia as I recall my childhood dump rake adventures, happily navigating nowhere for hours at a time. And then the colors catch my eye—the golds, the yellows, the oranges—from the pale tan straw and corn shocks to the pumpkins, gourds and squash, the sun-bright mums, and the flannel-shirted scarecrow, all arranged in and around the old rake with its tall steel wheels. It is a fine still life for a country boy.

I am being self-centered. Never mind just me, Denny and Linda have done our whole family a favor. Just today as we returned home from a matinee it was all eyes left and smiling as we surveyed their autumnal yard art installation. When we pulled into our own yard we were still talking about the beauty of the arrangement —not that it was so marvelous or ornate, or refused to be ignored in the manner of your gaudier Christmas displays, but rather how the time Denny and Linda took to decorate their yard wound up providing us with a moment of aesthetic pleasance (although none of us actually uttered the words "aesthetic pleasance" and in fact just generally agreed that it was good to have neighbors like Denny and Linda, who, beyond artful pumpkin placement also do our chicken chores when we go on vacation) in the midst of the day-to-day hustle. All week long as we rush back and forth from work, from meetings, from school drop-offs and play practice and getting the groceries, there is always that moment as we slow to turn up our hill that we get to enjoy the full beauty of the well-adorned dump rake, a moment of neighborly order, peace, and beauty, ours for the looking as the landscape colors itself up to match. The weather has been gray, but we enjoy the bright blessing of good neighbors.

BARNYARD BALLET

As both patron and purveyor of the arts I participate whenever possible and this morning I gave the world a ballet. It was your bad luck to miss it.

This jewel of the dance was born of incessant rain (a meteorological and metaphorical reality for weeks now) and bad shoes. My mind was preoccupied with the state of the world and the sogginess of our basement as I made the walk beneath the apple tree toward the chicken coop to release and feed the poultry. There was the spat-spat of raindrops in the leaves above me and the squish-squish of the sodden lawn beneath me, and my spirit was in a mood to match. Self-pity is a pernicious little tincture but then the jokes have to come from somewhere.

On the upside, I had an early start on the day. A quick round of chores, and then up to the office above the garage, a generally carbon-neutral commute to do my part to keep the economy doing whatever it's doing. If nothing else, I am good at trudging. Plodding. Been doing it for years now. And no matter my mood, it always brightens when I dump the chicken bucket (specifically, a plastic ice cream pail filled with eggshells, table scraps, plate scrapings, and an assortment of cores, peels, and spoilage), as only a stone statue could straight-face the entertainment provided when the cackling horde sets upon the refuse, the first step in a marvelous alchemy ultimately manifesting in a frittata.

So I was neither high nor low, just in-between and going about my business. The persistent precipitation has created a muddy slick just inside the chicken fence, and I made a mental note of it as I approached. As ever, "mental notes" are fun to review after the fact.

The relevance of the mud slick was amplified by my aforementioned shoes; rubberized clogs with no discernible tread. I was also wearing gray socks, bad shorts, and a shapeless hoodie. This ensemble reflects my deference to art; you don't want the beauty of the dancer to distract from the dance.

The way I cross the fence is I sidle up to it, swing my left leg up and over like I'm on a kick line for people who don't like to kick, then pivot and follow with the other. As I swung my left leg, I confirmed the muddy conditions and thought, "Better be careful." Similar to my "mental notes," these thoughts rarely influence the subsequent action, which is why, as I swung my right leg to follow, my left foot shot out from beneath me, I achieved a position of horizontal levitation familiar to anyone who's ever slipped on the ice, then dropped to the muck in a thudding heap. There followed a brief moment of contemplation broken by the light patter of chicken bucket bits dropping commingled with cold rain upon my face.

That would sell some tickets, I thought. Sadly there was no audience. Not even the chickens, still locked in their coop. Sometimes we dance alone, our art an invisible ripple through the universe. Sometimes we begin the day in unexpected ways, standing naked in the laundry room.

GARLIC AGAIN

The wind is stripping the last color from the trees. The yard is alive with the rattle and scatter of leaves. After a gray morning the clouds cottoned up and let the sun cut through. The thermometer took a ten-degree bump, but there is sharpness to the light, a message from the near future, where the sun gives us nothing but a snow-blind squint.

Poetic considerations aside, we have to get the garlic in. Shortly I will bring the tractor 'round, drop the tiller and stir up the dirt, which we'll shape into linear mounds. Then, one-by-one, we'll poke the cloves into their rows, back into the same earth from which they emerged earlier this summer, when the air was hot and heavy and everyone was hunting shade and lemonade. Now it's boiled dinner and board games around the woodstove.

Yesterday as I drove my younger daughter home from school, she said autumn was her favorite season. I take this to mean she has an old soul, or at least she's way ahead of me. When I was her age I was still stuck on summer. Mainly because I didn't like cold weather, and without school the days seemed endlessly open. In my teens I expanded my appreciation for spring, but this was attributable almost entirely to unrequited hormones and poetic pretensions leading to a lot of staring out my bedroom window when I should have been cleaning the calf pens.

It wasn't until adulthood that I began to appreciate autumn, largely as a glide-path to winter. A buffer between beach balls and blizzards. A time for reflection and preparation. A cornucopia of symbolic and metaphorical pegs upon which to hang your scribbler's cap once you've realized spring favors fools. But I am glad my daughter has come to love autumn early, as so much of this life is predicated on impermanence and the fall season is all that and a pumpkin.

Sometimes a paragraph break equals 24 hours. I report back now to say we got a late start on the garlic and finished under moonlight. At least that's how the romantic springtime version of me would have put it. The autumnal me, scolded to truth by the clatter of dead cornstalks, is compelled to explain that the lunar phase didn't quite deliver enough glow to go, so I ran a 40-foot extension cord from the house and rigged an LED shop light so we could complete the job by bedtime. And in the category of Parents Are Always Learning, I discovered that outfitting a fading grade-schooler with a headlamp invests dread chores with a sense of just enough adventure to make it across the finish line.

Today's wind is stiffer than yesterday's. When I stepped out to do chicken chores a cyclone of leaves blew through door and dropped in the porch. Perfect conditions then, to inspect the garlic mounds, infused with cloves from end-to-end, blanketed in a layer of leaf mulch and another of straw, each straight row staked beneath an unrolled stretch of orange plastic safety fence, this last an unpoetic element, but necessary to keep the chickens from digging things up and hold the leaves and straw in place so the cloves can meditate into winter while the world blows by.

STICKY DRUM

The bottom of the 55-gallon drum we use to store chicken feed finally rusted through. For once in my life I was prepared. I had a dozen replacement barrels down in the pole barn. I can't remember how I obtained them. It might have been in the early 2000s, right after we moved to the farm and I dove deep into the world of auctions (online and off), Craigslisting, and literal dumpster-diving (specifically at convenience store construction sites)(you should see my collection of pristine bricks in a pristine pile with no pristine idea what to do with them for years now) (occasionally I prop something up).

I had a lot of plans. I'm not sure what happened to the plans, but I still have a lot of stuff. If you are interested in 500 feet of green plastic tubing that never quite became the underground pig-watering system of my dreams, just drop me a note and prepare to spend a little time in the weeds.

It also occurs to me that the steel drums may have come via my buddy Mills, who is, um, well, let's call it a professional-grade *collector*. Mills hits auctions like an osprey hits fish. Except the osprey stops after one fish, and doesn't ever jump out behind a bush wearing plastic hillbilly teeth. Beyond the bidding Mills is a barterer and wheeler-dealer supreme. He'll trade you anything, he can get you anything. Just yesterday I received a text from a recording engineer hunting a truckload of sawdust. I didn't ask why, just texted back, "I know a guy," and within five minutes Mills wrapped the deal.

Anyways, I went down to grab one of those barrels and was pleased to discover they were in like-new condition. They were sealed, so before I opened the one I chose I checked the label, just to be sure I wasn't triggering a hazmat surprise. After googling "soy lecithin" I deemed it safe to proceed, and removed the lid.

Here's the problem. Commercial soy lecithin is like a combination of Vaseline and molasses. There was a residual inch in the bottom of the barrel. I tried scraping it, I soaked it in water overnight, and finally left the black barrel upended in two days of sun hoping the goo would melt and run out.

No luck, and it won't fit in the dishwasher. I did google "how do I wash out a barrel of soy lecithin" and within 30 seconds was scrolling through the world of survivalist forums. In my own sweet way I like to think I too am a survivalist, but based on what I read there I lack the requisite seriousness. And so it was back to the maybe-survivable world, where without the aid of a search engine it occurs to me that dish soap will probably do it, although in what amount I don't know, and a pressure washer might be in order. I don't have a pressure washer, but I know a guy, and he just might let me rent it for the low, low, price of 500 feet of green plastic tubing...

DAD SUIT

There is a wedding in the offing. Someone dear to the family, and I have a small role in the proceedings. Thus there has been launched a project to dress me in a manner a few notches above my usual look, best described as absent-minded roadie wandered out to chop wood in a free T-shirt. The project is being overseen by my in-house fashion consultants, otherwise known as my wife and daughters.

I have a suit. One suit. And although I worked real hard to put myself in a position where I need never wear that suit, I do defer to respect and honor when it comes to weddings and funerals. Trouble is, I bought that one suit to get myself married in, and in the years since passed, it no longer conveys my unique sense of style in the manner I prefer, which is to say boy the pants really pinch at the waist there, and the suit-coat buttons are located a little too far from the buttonholes, and if at any point during the ceremony I have to kneel, it will be a tensile-testing moment for that rearmost seam.

So there have been a series of shopping expeditions—both online and off—and corresponding "fashion shows" in which Dad does laps from the bathroom to the living room, where a panel of three judges reclines upon the couch to make noises and gestures of approval or disapproval and sometimes just snort. I am built on the order of a lumpy stump, so the perfect fit is elusive. It's an architectural problem, really. Plus, I'm cheap, so we're pretty much working off the rack, and the discount rack at that.

As of now we have it narrowed down to two pair of pants, two pair of dress shoes, and maybe that one shirt. There has been one fruitless trip to the suit jacket section, general confusion over ties, and a truckload of returns. I have also been told my gray tube socks won't make the cut, not even the ones without holes. So there will be hosiery sessions.

I will let you in on a little not-so-secret. I *really* don't like wearing suits. And I'd rather clean the chicken coop all day on a hot day wearing nothing but jorts and sandals than go suit shopping for one single hour. But the "fashion show" part? Where Dad inevitably slips from sullen or stern to silly? Maybe even does some catalog poses, or a twirl? Where the jury spends as much time giggling as reviewing? And how in the end they render me presentable and we take a nice family picture at the wedding reception? In those moments I know full well I may be a willful schlump, but I am a blessed schlump. Those fashion show giggles and clowning add up and establish reserves to be drawn on in tougher times. Times when you need threads woven of something more metaphysical than the threads they're dressing me in to take my turns up and down the roughneck catwalk in the very heart of our home, where I must take care not to vogue too near the wood stove, or, as a matter of situational irony, step on the cat.

BIG BUCK

Today a buck deer sporting headgear of a height and breadth sufficient to cradle your average Packers fan showed up outside my office. I had stepped out to test the air and startled a doe on the lawn. It is courting season for the local ungulates, and I figured there might be a buck about, so I approached the wooded verge and there about forty yards deep in the birches spotted a mobile hat rack of a size that causes my neighbors to huddle over their cellphones during intermission of the school concert as everyone compares snapshots uploaded directly from their game cameras.

In this case I have no photos, so you'll just have to take my word for it, and it's fine if you don't, because as big as he was I've seen bigger, and you can take that down to the café and multiply it by three. Plus who trusts digital images in these our manipulated and conspiratorial times? I'm satisfied with the image in my mind. Also, ten minutes from here, it is not unusual to spot bucks of similar stature posing beneath the city limits sign, grazing in suburbia, or trying to sneak between the Kwik Trip and the car wash.

Still, I retain just enough rural Wisconsin DNA to react to

the sight of a big buck—be it in the woods or over the hood—
with an innate thrill. Some of it is undeniably predatorial. I
was raised in a hunting culture, all culminating in that stretch
of days some call Holy Week, when school, schedules, and all
but the most essential chores, were suspended from dusk to
dawn while we tromped the swamps, sat in trees, and hoped
against hope we might happen into The Big One, which
would give us bragging rights for a few days when school
resumed. Nowadays pursuit of the Big One is based less on
hope than technology, but then so is Christmas shopping.

But it is the sense of hope—cousin in this case to wonder,
and certainly linked to my rural youth—that extends the
thrill of seeing a big buck beyond the idea of "taking" it.
When as a boy I bumbled 'round the forest, it was rare to see
a deer, let alone a buck, and even rarer to see a big buck. This
is due to a combination of factors, not the least among them
the fact that I was not exactly the stealthiest knucklehead
afoot, and unable to sit still for long. Nonetheless, when I'd
sight an antler of any size, it was exciting, and to this day the
sight triggers the same nerve path.

This nerve also hits me in the arms. This too is traceable
to the days of my youth, when Dad swerved the headlights
toward any pair of glowing eyes in hopes of seeing a pair of
antlers perched above them. To this day if we are off the four-
lane, the sight of illuminated deer eyes causes me to involun-
tarily yank the wheel and point the high beams at whatever's
out there lest it be ol' Mossy Rack. My family (my wife in
particular, who was raised without this obsession) makes
unhappy noises when I do this. Perhaps the whiplash has
given them a pain in the neck. Perhaps the pain in the neck is
perched in the driver's seat, ogling ungulates.

WEDDING DANCE

It was that stage of the wedding dance when all of the neckties—and a few hairdos—had gone loose. Some of the older aunts and uncles were gathering their coats, a spraddle-legged father sat cradling a toddler asleep against his collar, and the desserts table was devastated, but the dance floor was full and thumping, young to old.

As I surveyed the scene from beside a table of empties and half-empties, it occurred to me how the impression and import of a wedding shifts with perspective. Leaving aside the obvious significances for the couple featured, I thought instead of the pre- and gradeschoolers, for whom the day must seem a mix of pageant and play-acting, culminating in being allowed to eat sugar and run in the house; bound of course to end in a crash, but worth every giddy bit of it. For the middle-school and teen set, it is training grounds for carrying themselves in adult forms of celebration, a chance to experience new formalities absent the pressures of the homecoming dance. For the emancipated singles it is a full-on blowout, an occasion for hope or despair or confirmation, and—in the case of at least one of my newest relatives—a chance to not only loosen his tie but wear it as a headband. For the elderly and wise, perhaps a chance to share a smile for youth, but also for being past all that.

For the participant parents, the day is a stew of hope and joy seasoned with unease and sadness; the relief of responsibilities discharged leavened by worries and uncertainty. In other words, parenting as it ever is.

Finally, for those of us toiling through the middle (we assume) stages of marriage, much of what we feel depends on how things are going. Speaking for myself there is a renewal of gratitude for my wife and all she has given me, for all the ways she has bettered (as opposed to *bested*, although you would not be wrong) me, for the ways she allows me another shot at the runway when I land short, and that she lets me dance with her even though I pretty much can't. There are also more bracing thoughts, especially when confronted by the newlywed sparkle; when have I last seen that sparkle? When have I last *earned* that sparkle? Anything beyond that is between my wife and me—for better or worse.

And so we danced. By evidence and definition, I cannot do that verb, but those were not the standards of the evening, and so I hit the floor—and not just for the usual two slow ones with my wife. I herked and jerked and now and then tried to count it out, and did a very Scandinavian salsa merengue, but mostly I just joined in joy with the happily disheveled crew, some from near, some from far, some never met before and some never to meet again. The wedding was a ceremony for two; this second ceremony—of cellphones forgotten face down amidst the crumpled napkins, of high heels kicked to the corner, of pulsing light and sound while outside the world spun round—was for everyone in the couple's orbit, doing our best no matter how flat our feet to dance two people happily into the future.

SAUSAGE TIME

Find your happy place, they say, and so I am cutting up venison in the living room while watching the Packers. This is an annual tradition requiring a folding card table, a forgiving carpet pattern and an understanding spouse. It also speaks to a certain relaxed approach to existence in general and food processing in particular. Life in rural Wisconsin is glorious.

Despite the touchdown celebrations and demonstrative exhibitions of despair, somehow I still have all my fingers. I have suffered two minor lacerations to each hand, but neither as a result of the current multitasking. I incurred the first while skinning a deer in the pole barn, the second while I was washing the first wound in the sink while holding the knife in my mouth by its handle. Reaching for a towel, I somehow ran my previously uninjured hand across the blade of the knife clenched in my choppers. Upon hearing the story, some of my closest relatives asked what I was thinking and I have no answer although I appreciate them assuming that thinking had anything to do with it.

In certain social circles I suppose the idea of butchering wild game in the parlor would wrinkle a nose or two, but just see if I give *them* any sausage. Furthermore the woodstove is roaring right along just over there, and just as we worked to stack up a winter's worth of firewood I am working to store up a year's worth of protein. The fact that I choose to do so while watching Aaron Rodgers loft laser spirals across a high-def flat screen does not dilute my pioneer spirit.

The game is not going well. I trust the Packers are trying their best, although it's been a less than soaring season. There is always hope when you have a quarterback named Rodgers or Favre, so even when things aren't stellar I reflect on the eras of Dickey and Dilweg and Tomczak and Randy Wright, and am grateful for the highlights that have come our way since 1992. Above all, the Sunday drama helps pass the time when the thrill of hand-carving artisanal venison chunks has dissipated.

Winning is better than losing, but the state of Green Bay's conference record or playoff chances has no discernible effect on our family freezer, so no matter the outcome of tonight's tilt, next Tuesday my buddy Mills will come over and he and my wife and I will grind and mix and shoot the breeze and test the sausage in a cast iron pan in real time. These ceremonies will take place in the kitchen, not the living room. There are limits, and the Packers don't play on Tuesday. In fact, football may not come up at all. Gotta keep your eye on the ball or the breakfast patties run heavy to nutmeg.

And so I carve and watch as the game winds down, happy to live in the land of Green and Gold, grateful for our locally-sourced back forty bounty, and in the morning as the light of day streams through the windows I will give that carpet a good going-over.

THE PIANO TUNER

This week the piano tuner visited. I don't know a lot about piano tuning other than you don't want me tuning yours. I know you need a good ear and some wrenches. And I wonder if it's a dying art, as pianos are a dying instrument, if an article I read six years ago remains relevant. The reporter wrote that piano sales were plummeting. Many reasons were given, from all the songs you'd ever want to hear being available on your phone to the lack of support for music education in schools. The market for used pianos was so anemic recyclers were smashing them with sledgehammers and trucking the pieces to the dump.

There was always an old upright piano in the farmhouse of my childhood. Dad would plink away at hymns after we were in bed, and he could also bang out a rollicking version of "On Top of Old Smoky" that belied his otherwise pedestrian playing. I used to pedal my bike around our country block to take piano lessons from Mrs. North, but while she was able to train me up to the point of playing "Let There Be Peace On Earth" at the elementary school Christmas concert, football soon became more interesting than scales, and I haven't played formally since.

Our elder daughter took piano lessons for years and has recently resumed playing in hopes of obtaining a college music scholarship, an endeavor I support for reasons of culture and finance. The first piano we bought for her to practice on was some Russian knock-off prone to rapid detuning. At some point we sold it for not much money and part of the deal was that my buddy Zeus and I had to move it. It was a struggle but we were successful, which means that counting the time my Swiss expatriate pal Beat and I moved a piano way more than we expected, I am one for two in moving pianos without breaking them. That's 50% better than my farmer pal Al, who once begged and wheedled a piano from the local elementary school music teacher for a beer-based small-town talent show by promising he would personally ensure its safe return, a promise broken when he looked in his rear view mirror and saw the piano pin-wheeling down Highway 8, leaving a trail of kindling. Eventually Al would admit his commitment to celebration had exceeded his commitment to securing the piano to the trailer.

Our current piano has a light on it that alerts us when it is thirsty, which happens a lot in the winter season when the woodstove is cooking along just across the living room. Today I stand in front of the crackling fire and listen for a moment as the tuner pings and adjusts the strings. When I was young and courting a girl in the church of my youth, we would gather around a piano with other teens of a Sunday after-noon and sing hymns in harmony. It was a simpler time, or at least I remember it so. Today my younger daughter—who has had a few lessons but mostly improvises—records her homemade songs directly from the piano to an iPad. I have taught her very little about how to navigate the keyboard, although to complete this little shaggy dog roundup of piano recollections, I did hide her Easter basket in the cabinet once, just like my Mom did for me. Perhaps this hastened the need for a tune-up.

CONTRAILS

At dawn I saw contrails lain parallel across the sky and thought of cross-country ski tracks. This reflects cultural bias and December in rural Wisconsin and—now that I think of it —the fact that I used my wife's skis to wedge the basement door shut last evening in order to keep the cats down there overnight and out of leftovers stored on the porch.

This is one of those pieces written well prior to its printing. I'd love to attribute the timeline to proactive overachievement; rather it's a reflection of holiday printing schedules and my editor requesting I help people who show up to work hard at real news every day catch a rare break. In light of history unfolding at the speed of Tweet, there is this sense that every phrase I type, every word, will be post-loaded. What if I compose an ode to puppies and lollipops only for the ode to hit print the day after someone stabs a puppy with a lollipop? Or nominates a lollipop to a cabinet position? (I vote for a puppy.)

So I write oblivious to the future present and return to today's day, which broke bright but frozen, the sky clear save a few skipping-stone clouds, which by the time I hauled the water bucket to the chicken coop were seared red and golden on the underside. The twin contrails cut unnaturally through them on an east-west line, left by big jets beginning the descent to Minneapolis. I saw the thin strips of condensation as both metaphor and intrusion, and thought how the person feeding chickens when our farmhouse was built in the 1880s never encountered such a sight, and briefly wondered what percentage of the couple hundred people propelled by the residual exhaust were fleeing the present as opposed to pursuing the future. Then I stepped on a knob of frozen chicken poop, which, like the princess' proverbial pea, redirected my eyes and attention to the more relevant elements of the day at hand.

The chickens were voracious as always, pecking their way through each other to get at the feed, but I spare myself and you this particular metaphorical sidetrack to say that after I got their water topped off I stopped for a moment on the snow-pack path between the house and the coop to absorb the ongoing sunrise. For a moment the world was aligned, the sun burn-bleeding through distant stripped poplars to rise over the spine of the back forty, the ridge inscribed with ski tracks cut by my wife during yesterday's foray, the matched white ribbons a grounded mirror image to the airliner residue fading above. It being near the end of the year I began to float off into the idea of time and symmetry and the human desire for a clear path through confusion, and then, startled by the crow of a particularly nasty rooster, I simply settled for the idea of returning to the work at hand and putting those skis back before someone trips over them.

CHRISTMAS TREE INJURY

Nothing launches you full bore into the newborn day like piercing your big toe with a Christmas tree needle. The fuzziness of night dissipates with the suddenness of a flash-bang grenade. No matter how glorious the sunrise, it cannot compete with the galvanizing effect of the transdermal introduction of wood products into this or that little piggie. You obtain absolute focus. Exercise, also, as you drop like you've been shot, grabbing your socked foot on the way down, tuck-and-rolling off to moan in the half-light beside the couch like some lumpy Olympic tumbler who overshot the pommel horse, and, for that matter, the mat. If you are lucky you will not be carrying coffee.

Every year we swear we will water the Christmas tree daily, and every year we do for at least one day in a row. There are also the nefarious cats, who, despite two designated water bowls AND a toilet, linger thirstily about the base of yon Tannenbaum, waiting until you do remember to top off the receptacle within the stand, at which point they leap in to lap it all up, apparently preferring water infused with the flavor of a cheap gas station air freshener. It isn't that cats are evil, it is that they are evil in so many ways.

The watering process is its own sort of gauntlet, similar to those exercises where soldiers wriggle under barbed wire, only without the live fire—although getting drilled in the earhole by the pipe-cleaner halo of a fallen corn cob angel seems a relevant subcategory. Among the sounds of Christmas our children will harbor forever in their hearts are those emanating from the invisible top half of whoever's legs those are sticking out from beneath the boughs. From somewhere in there near the stump region arise curses, whimpers, trickles, spills, and splashes, visible anger fumes, and sometimes a request for Band-Aids. Watering the Christmas tree is the number one dread holiday chore, but because we are a close-knit family we take turns avoiding it.

The result? Medical-grade needles with all the pliability of titanium stalactites, and a shed rate that puts those cats to shame. It's like an organic acupuncturist has been seeing clients carelessly in the living room. Cross the room socked or barefooted and you are advised to strap on twin tweezer holsters.

When the tree—minus half its needles—is finally lugged to the fire pit, I'll miss it. We will shake out the skirt, return the stand to its box in the garage, and then we will vacuum and vacuum and vacuum. But the needles are profuse and the carpet is tenacious, and based on previous experience, I know there will come a morning—perhaps as late as next July—when I will shuffle bleary-eyed into the fresh dawn only to lurch airward in the manner of a break-dancing musk ox, and as I crash to the floor while clutching my foot, declare in all the spirit of the season, "Merry Christmas to all, and to all a @#$%..."

FAUX FOX

The fox was in stalking mode—head down and extended, tail the same but pointed straight opposite—and pacing toward the chickens clustered beneath the coop. Without hesitation I leapt from my desk.

I wasn't sure I'd get there in time. My office is located above the garage a good hundred yards from the pending crime scene. Furthermore, the office door is to the rear of the garage. I thundered across the room, slammed the door open and blasted through, then hung a tight downhill left. Picking up speed as I crossed the driveway, I realized I didn't really have a plan other than to wave my arms and holler. I was also rediscovering that I've never really been very good at sprinting, especially while wearing slippers, one of which is cobbled with duct tape. I don't so much stride as thud. We'd had a warm stretch so all the snow was gone, but the ground had refrozen and it was rough going in those slippers, compounded by some awkward toe-dancing betwixt the mole tunnels hard as galvanized pipe.

All this time I had been out of visual contact with the chicken coop. I would have to run clear 'round the house and out under the apple tree before I could see it. Envisioning the fox sprinting for cover with one of our layers flapping in its jaws, I reached down to grab another gear and nearly blew a slipper and a hammie, ultimately a wasted effort in that there was no other gear.

To say I run like a farmer is to insult a lot of farmers, but the prototype I picture is based on the agriculturists of my youth, who could work all day but were built for neither speed nor aesthetics and ate quite a bit of bologna. And in fact by the time I rounded the house and set my sights on clearing that apple tree, my form was that of a man jogging while carrying two pails of milk shortly after eating a lard sandwich.

But the chickens! I must save the chickens! This is what the brave farmer does! And thus I came BigFooting it out into the open ready to do battle, to pursue, to brave tooth and claw in defense of feather and beak. With heaving chest and assassin's eyes I scanned for the beast, and...and...

Nothing but a cat. An orange cat. Fur the shade of a fox.

Our cat. Just last night I was scratching the back of this cat as it lay on the couch upon which I had foresworn it would never set paws.

In my defense, I had been staring at a rough draft on a computer screen for a couple of hours before eyeballing the faux fox. Also, just last week I told my wife it was getting time for me to visit the ophthalmologist. This seals that deal. I returned to the office and my work, although not before stopping in the house to share the story with my wife, for if I cannot take her breath away by majesty I can give her giggle fits via my myopia.

AUDITIONS

Among the ways one proves one is serious about parenting is to spend the second half of one of the better professional football playoff games of the year helping an 11 year-old fill out audition forms at the local children's theater. While the two teams matriculated the ball up and down the field, I sat beneath anemic fluorescents, cross-referencing my phone calendar with laser-printed notes from my wife and a form provided by the director to establish what scheduling conflicts might exist should the child get a part in the play. It wasn't exactly 4th and long with the season on the line, but you could say I was playing under pressure.

I wasn't the only one. The room was a teeming cluster of nervous youngsters and their parents. Everyone walks through the door knowing there aren't enough parts to go around. It's a relatively close-knit community and the ratio of excited hugs and hellos to stage-parent maneuvering tips heavily to the happy side of things, but still there are vicarious butterflies.

Life is filled with casting calls whether we're aware of it or not, so I'm glad my child has an interest in the footlights. It's good prep for being rejected by the insurance company or a date or fate itself. It has taught her the importance of giving your all in every role, and how much you can learn from the wings. And in those cases where she was fortunate enough to land a larger role, there is the idea of leadership as a position in which the most critical responsibilities exist outside the spotlight: Learn your lines, hit your mark, make difficult things look easy, and if someone else forgets their lines, be prepared to ad lib in such a way that no one in the audience has a clue. Anybody can *play* the lead; can you *be* the lead?

Still, I really wanted to watch that football game. Especially when I managed to sneak a peek on my phone just long enough to learn that a spectacular comeback was underway. Yet I didn't dare be the only parent in the place staring at my phone, giving out the occasional yelp or chair-juke. I say "only parent" because while one doesn't wish to trade in stereotype, the number of folks at theater tryouts who are really into the NFL is, I venture to say, *slimmish*, although once while sneaking a Thursday night game on my phone while waiting for dress rehearsal to release, another father I had long known to be nothing but liberally artful slid into the seat beside me and, whispering in desperate joy, said, "You got the *game?!?!?*" Come to think of it, the fellow who was filing out the audition sheet across the table from us was wearing a Packers cap, so already my thesis crumbles.

I peeked again while she was in the actual audition. The score was tight. Then my daughter reemerged and I snapped the phone off. As we crossed the dark parking lot to the car she took my hand, and in that moment I cared neither who got the win nor who got the part, only gratitude for the role of a lifetime: father, no script available, no spotlight required.

ECLIPSE

It was a school night, but the child was up and ill, so we stepped outside into the subzero stillness and stared up at the super blood wolf moon in eclipse. Then I gave her some cough medicine and put her back to bed.

There is an afghan on our couch that was crocheted by my grandmother on my mother's side. If I recall correctly she gave it to me as a high school graduation present. I know it was in my possession during my college years because in those times I was driving a 1951 International Harvester pickup truck that was as much rust as truck and fitted with a heater that couldn't melt butter in a tanning booth, which is why I used to drive with that afghan across my knees, which is how it came to have a dark stain from the time it came in contact with the black-greased base of the four-on-the-floor shift lever. Decades and many washings later, the stain has lightened and blended into the blue yarn so I can't find it anymore.

Grandma was an understated powerhouse of a grandma, ever clad in modest church-lady dresses with her hair up in a bun, even as she jumped rope into her 70s and outshot all comers during informal family reunion marksmanship contests. In one legendary session she left a particularly braggadocious son-in-law with an empty rifle in every sense, shaking his head over the tattered state of her bulls-eye as opposed to his relatively undisturbed own. A man of misplaced pride, he never spoke of it again. In her dying days she stayed with my mother, and drew her last breath with all her daughters present in the farmhouse. My younger daughter never met her, but the elder will tell you she remembers sitting on the edge of the eventual deathbed, visiting happily.

The afghan survived my truck and my bachelorhood and is now a fixture on the family couch or the floor adjacent. You will find it wadded more than folded, which is to say our housekeeping isn't always up to snuff but that old yarn is being used the way Grandma intended. To warm my wife and me as we watch football, to warm the child snuggled with a book, to warm family and guests assembled in our drafty family room. This includes cats and lately, boyfriends. All respectful fellows so far, but sometimes it'd be nice to have Grandma back, just sitting over there in a rocking chair with her rifle.

I had been reading a little too much late night news when the young one came downstairs tonight in tears and suffering a resurgent ear infection. All those current events had me similarly symptomatic, if only spiritually. You look at the child and understand you don't have any red-hot answers. You just wrap her in an afghan descended from the hand of her matriarchal line and step outside to watch the moon disappear. Then, after medicine, you tuck her back abed, sending her to sleep with a promise that the moon will glow again. Back downstairs you stand at the window and stare at the mudded orb, hoping you are right.

GARDEN MASTER

Lately I have been trending dark and maudlin, which may be a reflection of our times, or, less complicatedly, a reflection of self-centered whininess, so today I will try to go for a laugh, even or especially at my own expense. Fortunately, last night it was 18 below and I spoke at a master gardening conference, so material is at hand.

The comic irony of addressing master gardeners on a winter's night when the mercury is polar negative is outweighed by the purpose inherent in their gathering. You needed only watch the participants hustle stiffly from their cars to the conference center to understand they were here not only to draw on the warm memories of soft soil, but to bank that heat and carry it forward until the sprouting season returns. These were the more forward-looking ants from Aesop's grasshopper fable, gathering this winter to prepare the stores of next winter. They were preparing to prepare meals to be eaten a year from now. Currently their gardens were as hard as the asphalt lot where the motor oil in our parked cars had gone to taffy before we even got our name tags, but what better time to talk gardening than when you can't do gardening?

Speaking of "can't do gardening," there I was. I spoke from the heart, and I spoke from incompetence. The heart part grew mostly from my childhood memories; of the sound the wooden row marker made as Dad dragged it through the fluffy soil, the crisp crack of a carrot freshly rinsed beneath the hose tap, the sound of squash leaves moving in a warm breeze, the slow reveal surprise as the contents of the annual "mystery seed packet" cracked the dirt and reached for the sun and gave up their identities through the shape of their leaves. And more recently, the asparagus patch that sprouts as an annual living reminder of my wife and her prescience, as it was she who planted it while I was procrastinating elsewhere.

Then we arrived at the incompetence portion of the presentation. As an adult my love of gardening has been hamstrung a lack of discipline, patience, and production. As I described my misadventures—ordering seeds based on impulse rather than hardiness zones, assuming I could cause to emerge from the earth the same plants I saw in the catalog's pictures, planting the wrong plants at the wrong time in the wrong place—I hoped I was making these accomplished pros feel better about themselves. But I was also intrigued to see that even in a roomful of eminently accomplished gardeners, there was something in the laughter and nodding heads that spoke of recognition. Of that shared experience when nature gets the better of us. Afterward, when we shared stories informally, no one told me about the world-record tomatoes they'd grown; rather, they regaled me with the times things had gone delightfully wrong. Happy failure may be humanity's most undervalued trait.

Back in the parking lot I let our poor old van idle a bit before putting it in gear. The lot was nearly empty, the gardeners gone home or to hotels to bed. On the morrow they would return for a day filled by expert talk of raised beds, perennials, vegetable basics, bulbs, flowers and more. When the frozen earth unlocks itself they will be prepared, putting in practice horticulture as hope.

SAFE TRAVELS

This morning I sat beside my suitcase in the lobby of a big city hotel, waiting for a ride to the airport. Nearby, a group of people bid each other good-bye as their individual rides arrived. They interacted with a familiar and friendly air, but there were no hugs or demonstrations of affection that would indicate they were family. Rather it seemed they were dispersing from a work-related event.

One by one as each member departed, a woman who seemed somehow central to the crew sent them on their way with the phrase, "Safe travels!" They were a populous bunch, so she uttered the words again and again. Shortly I began hearing the phrase as mantra and drifted down a pleasant wormhole of reflection.

I remember adopting the phrase "Safe travels" a few decades ago, using it when a departure seemed grander or more significant than usual and deserving of more than the standard "See y'later," favored by my immediate family. "Safe travels," on the other hand, has a more sweeping, mythic feel. It also has the tone of something I would have picked up at a youth hostel while backpacking around Europe in the days when I was working hard at becoming more cosmopolitan.

This line of thinking led me to consider other forms of farewell, starting with that very word. Who in our day and age can say "Farewell!" without feigning a desperate swoon? Perhaps I am an immature goon. Your common and basic "Good-bye" always leaves me a shade nervous what with its intimations of finality. "Bye," on the other hand, may take parting too lightly, and uttered carelessly may sound dismissive. "Godspeed," it seems to me, should be reserved for persons embarking on especially critical or noble missions, as a posthumous honorific, or specifically humorous occasions, for instance when your neighbor Donnie decides to root out that septic tank problem once and for all.

I have learned that my Spanish-speaking relatives favor "Chao" over "Adiós" when it's time to hit the road. As I understand it, this is a matter of informality. Speaking of informality, I enjoy a nice "Catch ya on the flip-flop" every now and again, if for no other reason than to recall the memory of the man who taught it to me, my Uncle Stan the long-haul trucker. And perhaps my favorite valediction? The one the farmers of my youth uttered time and time again when milking time drew nigh: "Weellll...I s'pose..." Shortly thereafter, off we would go. Well, not so shortly, as where I'm from good-byes often take part in extended stages usually only terminating when the driver's side window goes up. In fact saying good-bye can be a journey in and of itself.

"Safe travels." The more she said it, the more I spun it around in my mind, the more it took on poetry and beauty. Two words, reminding me to never take for granted the precious the gift of surviving point A to point B. No matter the distance, we set out into uncertainty. "Safe travels," the stranger said, and off we went, our sails filled with a blessing.

CROWDSOURCED TRUCK REPAIR

I once wrote a column about our old plow truck and how every now and then it wouldn't start. Battery fine, fuel supply fine, but when I twisted the ignition key the truck either sat silent or cranked and cranked without firing. Three of my go-to mechanics were baffled (to say nothing of anyone I could corner at the café, the feed mill, and family reunions), and the standard interventions—new plug wires, distributor, fuel pump rehab, and so on—didn't fix the problem, which was all the more maddening for its intermittence. Symptom-free for months, then dead three times in a week, but never when it was in the shop. Most vexatious? Twice when it refused to start I had it towed to the mechanic, and the moment it was unloaded from the flatbed it fired up like it was fresh-bought off the lot.

These days all the cool people say crowdsourcing is the way to go, so I asked readers for help, and you responded. Some of the suggestions—replace the coil, check for a dead spot on the solenoid, vapor lock, gas cap issues, catalytic converter—were good ones, but had already been fed into the equation and eliminated via automotive algebra.

Some solutions were colorfully proposed, and wrapped in wit: "You may have a relay with an independent streak." "Wanna sell it for $500?" "Cut your losses and get rid of that boat anchor and get a new truck, preferably a great big one that you need a step ladder to get in." To the specialist who suggested "ball peen hammer to the solenoid," I promise I was way ahead'a ya on that one.

Meanwhile, the mechanic and I had a meeting in which we reviewed all the remaining treatment options, cross-referenced by my checkbook. We settled on replacing the computer module. Believe it or not a '94 Silverado has one, and several readers had pointed in that direction, some referring to it as the "black box." The plan was to get a used module, which would save some dollars. If that didn't resolve the issue, we'd pull the plug for good.

I'm happy to report we didn't even get that far. In the process of removing the old computer, the mechanic discovered an obscure little wire that had rusted through in such a way that every now and then it wiggled out of contact. All that trouble, down to a few pennies worth of conduction. He replaced the wire, I didn't have to pay for a replacement computer unit, and the truck has started and run fine ever since.

Until this week. The four-wheel-drive failed during a major snowstorm. More specifically, while my wife was plowing and I was 1,700 miles away in a state full of sun and cacti. Friends and neighbors came to the rescue, but that truck may be in more trouble than it knows. If the problem can be solved with WD40 and a ball peen hammer, it will live on. If not, it will be allowed one two-wheel-drive trip to the mechanic, where we will run the numbers specifically as they pertain to diminishing returns.

This time there will be no crowdsourcing. But I thank everyone who wrote. Whether or not you identified the problem, you joined me in the hunt. And the unifying theme was frustration, which really warmed my heart. Nothing makes me feel better in my bafflement than knowing others— including others far more mechanically-inclined than I—are suffering the same blood pressure spikes. We are in this together. Or so I told my wife over the phone from Tucson.

THE AGE OF PICKLEBALL

During a recent visit to a warm state I fell into an offhand conversation about pickleball and learned I am now eligible for residence in certain communal enclaves based on my having passed a milestone we're just gonna round off and call "my mid-50s." It was one of those moments when you are unequivocally reminded that no matter how youthful you feel, as far as the Homeowners Association is concerned you are a well-traveled Buick. I wasn't troubled by the mortal reminder—all in all I'd rather pass milestones than kidney stones and in either case it's the gravestone that really gets ya —but it was bracing to find myself mentally cruising past a retirement community only to have the gatekeeper beckon and hand me a brochure.

There are a lot of factors that will have to fall into place before you'll find me on a saguaro-shaded pickleball court (although the icicles sprouting INSIDE our basement after the recent snow dump are needling me in that direction). First and foremost retirement itself is at this point neither possible nor possible. Then there is health insurance, an impending tuition situation, and possibly a new U-joint for the plow truck, all of which have budget precedence over my first liquid graphite pickleball paddle. Also, I will not be able to sell the farm and move until we arrange a week-long special with one of those reality TV shows where they come in and de-clutter your outbuildings with a backhoe, a fire-hose, and perhaps a stick of dynamite.

One participant in the retirement community conversation whose parents lived in a nearby establishment said the rules allowed for one family member under 50, which means we won't have to sneak my wife past the clubhouse in the trunk. This is good news because not only do I find the idea abhorrent, I'm not up to that level of wrestling, and she is. You would find me in the trunk rolled in a yoga mat and bound in Pilates straps.

If I have learned anything in this life it is never say never. There are times—during this recent trip, for instance—when I dip into lifestyles utterly unlike my own, and sometimes it feels just great to start a winter's day with sunscreen and a homegrown backyard orange rather than snotsicles and chicken chores. The time may come when I choose splitting the check for brunch over splitting another load of firewood.

I have conducted preliminary research on entry-level pickleball paddles. There is a facility fifteen minutes from our snowbound farm featuring heated indoor courts. I watched an instructional video and it seems like fun. I may give it a try, but I will not be going in full-bore. At my age you are not only eligible for age-based residential living, you have also developed a nose for the scent of a fad, and somewhere down in that impenetrable pole barn is a box filled with the mouse-nibbled remnants of the Early 1980s Racquetball Scare. That baby blew up and flopped in the time it would take you to say, "Pickleball!"

NOTE: The minute this piece hit print, I got emails in stern defense of pickleball. I like pickleball. Pickleball is terrific. I am pro-pickleball. May it thrive, and its players as well. But speaking as the proud owner of my own personal "cornhole" set, sometimes you gotta just swing the needle from serious to silly and revel in our delicious human absurdities.

GOTTA GUY

Wherein we revisit the saga of the detachable gas tank...

Having spent the previous three days criss-crossing the state at 70 miles per hour in a van full of books and music gear, I counted it a blessing that I was three miles from home and sitting still when the gas tank fell off.

It had been a trying day. For starters, when I fired up my laptop a puff of smoke emerged. It was if the hard drive had chosen a pope, and for his first trick he turned my computer into a brick. Off I went to the laptop hospital. Preoccupied with sad computer thoughts, I opened a garage door, hopped in the van, and backed into the garage door I had *not* opened. I didn't blast through it, but I warped it good. It took three karate kicks before it would raise.

The computer doctor confirmed a terminal diagnosis requiring transplant. I headed home in a mope. As I turned on to Schumacher Road I heard a *thump* from the back of the van. I drove on. A stray guitar amp, perhaps. Plus when you're rolling a 2002 Toyota BandVan, a *thump* ain't nothin'.

But then came a second *thump*. You get *two* thumps, the

second one louder, you gotta investigate. I eased to the shoulder and stepped out for a look.

At that very moment the gas tank dropped from the chassis and hit the asphalt.

While you entertain yourself with visions of my reaction, I'll cut ahead to me leaving a voicemail with Kris, our mechanic. With his business partner Justin, Kris operates out of a converted car wash, has never steered us wrong, aligns his recommendations with our budget, and—this is the best sign of all—can be tough to get on the phone because he's so busy. He's not "ours" of course, but we think of him as such because he is "gotta guy" certified, as in, "Yah, I gotta guy…"

"Can you reattach a gas tank?" I asked when Kris called back. I've learned to cut right to the chase. Kris is not about the chit-chat. "Yep," he said. "Did a couple last month. Just gotta order the straps."

I typed this column on the formerly smoking computer. That was a spendy fix, but well done and worth it. The garage door is still kinda bowed out there at the bottom, but goes up and down. The van has put on many thousands of miles since the tank graft took. I was just in to see Kris this week with our plow truck. He got the four-wheel drive working just in time to beat the blizzard. He and his crew were on a dead-run hustle, as usual. Good work gets you good work.

It occurs to me much is revealed about my character, the level of my achievements, and the nature of the vehicles I own, by my frequenting a mechanic who is commonly acquainted with the reattachment of gas tanks. I imagine sometimes what it would be like to call your higher-end service departments with the same request. Deal is, if the gas tank drops off your Escalade, gimme a call. I gotta guy…

SHOVELING SNOW WITH EDITH WHARTON

This whomper of a winter having rendered it nearly impossible to remain philosophical about shoveling snow, I went literal, running Will Durant's *The Story of Philosophy* through my earbuds while clearing the never-ending decks. The juxtaposition of hacking a path to the chicken coop in your sweaty earflappers while Henri Bergson declares, "for a conscious being, to exist is to change, to change is to mature, to mature is to go on creating one's self endlessly" helps elevate your purpose.

The Bergson line elicited memories of an Edith Wharton quote from the 1930s in which, regarding "modern languages and good manners," she said, "I have lived to see both those branches of culture dispensed with." In response, a contemporary critic wrote, "Mrs. Wharton belongs to a tradition which is ending. She realizes this, and surveys without asperity the succeeding chaos." Things change, says Edith. Relax.

Then there are those things that should change, but don't. So it is we find Wharton—in 1913—writing "a fierce indictment of the materialism that ruled America," and citing elements of society that "did not hesitate to abolish its standards while most loudly proclaiming them." This, as they say, rings a bell.

These tangents helped pass the shoveling time and braided nicely into a recurring thread of personal rumination concerning the state of the nation and my dedication to staving off brittle codgerism. Change is natural, necessary, and unavoidable; may I never block it out of uninformed fear or presumptive comfort. In 1920, another critic observed how in one of Wharton's books, "the younger generation comes in like fresh air. Mrs. Wharton is all for the new and against the old...she would never...fear youth knocking at the door." Lately I am in the same mood. I just hope these youngsters arrive in time.

Codgerism lurks, even in the youth. On the same day I was pondering 20th century European philosophy and 20th century American literature, I managed to squeeze in time for a little 21st century Twitter, whereupon I found a younger friend proclaiming, "today's music is repeating itself." "Welcome to middle age," I replied. "It has been ever so, and we should talk sometime." If we do, I will show him the aspersive things I wrote about country music in the 1990s. There I was, wrinkling my nose at Garth Brooks and "pop" country, hailing the New Traditionalists, and diving deep into "alt" country. Twenty years later the latest generation of purists sing the same refrain, as if Chet Atkins never put orchestra music on a Tammy Wynette record.

Let me come clean: I am better at throwing snow than throwing quotes. I recalled the Wharton words only because I had read them that very morning, and the only reason I can cite them now is I used a green highlighter. The associations I have drawn above are tentative and tenuous, but then this is a newspaper column, not a master's thesis.

The snow falls, we shovel it, more snow falls, we shovel it.

Wharton and Bergson remind us that even if we're experiencing the same old thing we don't have to be the same old thing. Meanwhile, down there in the coop, the chickens are pulling for you, if only to deliver their water and scratch.

SNOWSHOES

I have put the snowshoes to good use.

Discard immediately the vision of me zipped into a natty fleece and touring nature. While this qualifies as good use and the nation's spirit curdles for lack of it, we are talking about my life, not Instagram. Conjure instead the image of a wild-eyed Ahab tromping back and forth between two pole barns, reeking of kerosene, sweat, and desperation.

But those pole barns are still standing, and therein lies my gratitude.

The gratitude is real. I can take you on a short drive around the neighborhood and point out neighbors who weren't so fortunate. An acquaintance lost a barn and cattle. A local volunteer firefighter was killed while removing snow from atop his outbuildings. Jokes and humor are my go-to, but for legions of people this winter has inflicted real pain. And even should it melt tomorrow, it is not done with us yet.

The location, size, and construction of my pole barns precludes my safely clearing them by either standard means (Several folks suggested I buy a roof rake, but A) this is not a roof rake situation, and B) Dude, after living in Wisconsin for

54 years I own an *assortment* of roof rakes.) or amazing means (yep, I've seen all the nifty YouTube videos), and the last time I hired professionals, they gave it a try then gave up.

Instead I assembled a quartet of torpedo heaters, and then, armed with the harpoon of my—yes—*roof rake*, spent my rare home days stalking back and forth between my two white whales, wherein and whereupon I nursed the heaters and dragged snow from the eaves as it slipped to within reach, pausing only to eyeball the weather app and deliver impromptu rants against one of my Top Five nemeses, the "non-spill" fuel nozzle, which I contend was secretly designed by an international petroleum cabal to derail the environmentalism movement in the name of environmentalism, but that is a screed for another script and you'd be surprised who's with me on this.

But from this running battle I took one simple joy: the utility of those snowshoes. They are nothing fancy. Basic entry-level model. Aluminum frames, plastic webbing, simple straps. Hardly your arctic racers. Nor are they heirloom-quality handcrafted wood-and-rawhide beauties worthy of being displayed on a ski lodge wall. But they do their job.

The snow hereabouts ranges from thigh-high to belly-high. A short trip to the granary for kindling is the equivalent of a cross-training session combining arctic exploration with snow-robics executed through a series of slogs and lurches. No wonder then, that I came to treasure the simple pleasure of taking a snow-shoed step and then another step without punching through the crust, without having to heave my hips forward and follow through with my thighs as a blunt instrument. I tromped, sure, but I was also floating above the earth. Walking on water.

I'm getting a little wild in the eye again. Obsession, kerosene fumes, and endless incoming piles of white stuff take their toll. But when dawn broke this morning the buildings were intact and the forecast predicted a week of thaw. Perhaps it is time to strap the snowshoes on one more time, tromp out and tour nature, then stand still out there in all that snow and say thank you.

WAFFLE KETTLE

Today's surprise announcement came courtesy of my telephone's amazing but imperfect ability to convert voicemails to text, which led to me staring into my palm at the transcription of a customer service representative's message declaring that as a means of resolving my concerns regarding their failed product "I do want to offer you a brand new waffle house...and I have two in mind that you might like."

How's that for a Tuesday?

Lower case or upper case, I was interested, although over the long term I'd prefer the latter, as it elicits fond memories of my days travel-writing through the American South via the trucking industry and country music bus drivers (the genesis of my art derives from a multifaceted palette). What a comfort it was, after driving all night, to see that simple yellow sign with the black letters as it hove into sight through the morning fog. Or across the parking lot from the no-tell motel when you pulled in peckish after midnight. There was dietary damage to be done, and waffles weren't the half of it. If you are raised country, you love to eat country.

Brand new, they said. So maybe they'll build it wherever I

wish? In that case, I'm thinking over there beside the granary. Across the yard, but close enough so I can catch a whiff of hash browns and bacon at break of day. I'll have my own booth, and maybe sneak in my own snooty coffee, but I won't mess with the menu.

Just now in the moment it occurs to me I'll also stroll over there every time I have to make a decision big or small, as based on my long history of deliberative flip-flopping, it would be pitch-perfect to do so with that sign glowing overhead.

If this is a straightforward franchising situation for an existing structure, I will negotiate my own parking spot out front and finance the second establishment, as I'd be getting two for one, life is Monopoly, and most clichés are based in fact, including "selling like hotcakes." Ingredients-wise, I have already cut the overhead by owning my own laying hens, and pigs can be arranged. I furthermore expect to expand profits by leveraging my contacts in the regional maple syrup community, starting with the neighbor who taps the two giant trees in our yard. Cut out the middleman, go straight tree-to-table, sit back and count the money.

It is at moments like these I wonder how it is I have yet to make my first million.

Followed immediately by the realization that this is exactly why I have yet to make my first million.

I regret to report I have now spoken with a live customer service representative. There will be no waffle house. Rather, I will be receiving a replacement electric kettle manufactured by a company whose name doesn't really sound like "waffle house" no matter what the phone heard. I'll make a fresh batch of coffee and get back to work on that million. Once a year I will use the new kettle to boil sap for syrup and imagine what might have been.

CUSTOMER SERVICE

I went ahead and spent good money on a pair of chore boots this week, high-top rubberized trompers with a cinch strap at the calf. Halfway through the first day I wore the boots, the clip designed to secure the excess cinch strap snapped. This made me cranky, and I went straight to the computer, fired off an email to the manufacturer, received a response within the hour from a representative who said I wasn't the only one experiencing this issue, they were contemplating a redesign, and they'd happily send me a replacement. A few days later a multi-pack of clips arrived in the mail, gratis. If I take perverse joy in relating customer service horror stories, it seems only fair that I own up to those instances when customer service is exactly what it claims to be.

No matter how steamed I am in these situations, I have learned to temper my initial approach. This is based on having more than once having rode into battle on my high horse, only to return afoot and wearing my own saddle when midway through the exchange it became clear the mistake was on my end, not theirs.

In many cases it is best to write what I call "refrigerator emails": write'em, let'em cool overnight, then delete in the morning. But sometimes the itch is too strong not to scratch.

Once upon a time our family used a certain company for certain services. Over a period of many years, the company performed terrifically. Then they got bought out or remade or somesuch. The "improvements" resulted in breakdowns and backlogs. Now then: As someone who sells things online and has dealt with his own customer service issues, I am slow to lambaste anyone because I know how dumb I feel when we mess up an order or someone has trouble accessing our site and I don't have the immediate fix. So I was pretty mellow about the problems and delays the company was experiencing. What finally tripped my trigger, what sent me snarkily to my keyboard was their repeated invocation – in emails and on recorded phone messages – of a certain phrase. And so, against my better judgment, I wrote them a note:

> *Also...may I politely and respectfully say that when someone tells me "We Love You" at every turn while apologizing for not being able to help me promptly, the effect is emotionally counterproductive? My helper had to hear it over and over while she was on an endless loop of hold with your customer service as well. I am a longtime satisfied and grateful client of [company]. I understand full well that changeovers often require patience, and I'm happy to give it. But seriously, this "we love you" stuff is a real load of Nutrasweet.*

And that was the fourth draft, with all the intemperate words removed.

It changed nothing, of course. I continued to receive regular assurances that [company] loved me, sometimes with an exclamation mark! This seems to be a theme with a lot of your contemporary online businesses, but I've never been a huggy guy, even less so when my credit card is involved. Just treat me straight and send me the boot clips; every time I pull my foot out of the mud and the boot comes with it, then, *then* I feel the love.

CHARACTER TEST

While navigating a street walled by snow and rutted with ice, I observed two young men with shovels attempting to free a car. This was back in the era of constantly digging out, which we easily recall as after two weeks of melt the slush piles still linger. As I drew nearer I recognized one of the individuals as a fellow of recent acquaintance. In the vernacular of another time, he had of late been calling on my daughter.

I have policies regarding such dudes: *Welcome to our house. Respect earns respect. We are not pals.* That said, the respect standard had thus far been met, so I pulled a U-turn and approached.

Current Dude—let's go with that, shall we?—looked up and recognized me. To his credit he did not flinch, but smiled and shook my hand. "Gotta get your car off the street before they tow it?" I asked. The city had been enforcing snow emergency rules. "It's not mine, it's his," said Current Dude, pointing to the other guy, now belting himself in behind the steering wheel. "I think we moved enough we can push him out," said Current Dude, sticking his shovel in the snow bank. I went around behind the car with him.

The snow was cleared, but the car's tires were sunk into the ice, and spun. Current Dude and I leaned into the trunk of the vehicle and began to rock it. Push, pause, push, pause, push...the key is in the timing. Push too soon, push too late, and you are fighting physics. We quickly got the rhythm, and were smooth in tandem. Vehicle-rocking is a genetic trait triggered by generational exposure to subzero temperatures and bald tires. It seemed a good sign this boy had it.

There is a point in the process when the sine wave of advance and retreat achieves an amplitude such that a single ounce of well-timed force will provide the momentum necessary to break the apex of the curve, and the car shoots free. We were almost there, so I adjusted my hand placement, increased the angle of my lean, drove hard with my legs, and shoved the heel of my hand right through one taillight. The car's spinning wheels caught the asphalt, the vehicle shot forward, and the driver accelerated out of sight.

By the look on his face, Current Dude wasn't quite sure what to say due to current respect parameters. Unfortunately the look on mine betrayed that I was perfectly aware of what I'd done.

"Man," I said, "when your friend gets back, tell him I'll take care of it."

"But I have no idea who he is," said Current Dude.

This was a twist.

Turns out Current Dude lives across the street, just happened to see the other fellow struggling, grabbed his shovel and went over to help. "Well, if whoever it was comes back and says you broke his taillight, you know where to find me," I said.

I figure that busted taillight drops my Good Samaritan rating to above "middling" but below "would recommend to a friend." Current Dude is still not my pal, but having caught him doing a good deed for a stranger, I declare respect earned and given.

CELLPHONE CONNECTION

As the insidious curses of hand-held (soon to be brain-contained) technology are widely documented, I'm gonna head in the other direction and say cellphones have worked out great for one very specific category of generally non-communicative rural Midwesterners: Me and my two brothers.

Jed (a logger) and John (a whatever-you-need but likely involving either a bulldozer, a rifle, or an airplane) (ask about his special 3-in-1 rate!) would not only be fine with my referring to them as Luddites, they cultivate the image—but each owns a cellphone. (One a flip model, and one a brand that pairs nicely with a latté, but that's as far as I'm going with this outing, as I still enjoy Thanksgiving.)

We three don't talk much. If one of us calls the other to wish a happy birthday, I guarantee you one of our wives handed us the phone. There is no family feud, it's just wiring. Our love and loyalty were long ago drop-forged in crisis. We feel little need for cards and affirmations. On the other hand, if it's dumb or goofy, we can't wait to share it. And while our lives and livelihoods have taken us in three different directions—certainly in occupation and sometimes in philosophy —thanks to those dumb phones we can be giggling in an instant.

Last month when I tried to spit through the face shield on my logger's helmet I immediately called one brother and texted the other—one so he could laugh at me and one so he could laugh *with* me. Did the same thing last November after I field-dressed and butchered three deer in one day without a single nick—only to jab my palm on the final cut, then, while washing out that wound, gash the thumb of my other hand with a knife I was *holding in my teeth*. Nothing mitigates pain and stupidity like a giggle-tears emoji forwarded by a logger in a forwarder.

There is also the fact—and this gets back to those differences in philosophy—that the impromptu sharing of off-kilter truths reaffirms our common perspectives. Thus when I see the headline "Man Injured After Shooting Self in Leg," I immediately call John, who answers with his dozer idling in the background. "I'm gonna read you a headline," I say, with no other preface, "and you tell me what's wrong with it." The instant I finish, he intones, "It should say Man Injured WHILE Shooting Self in Leg."

"*THANK YOU!*" I say, then, "See y'later!" And we hang up and that is it. My heart is lighter for an hour. It's the same when one of them rings me or pings me out of the blue with some oddity overheard at the implement store, or some knuckleheaded self-own at the timber landing.

I believe these little techno-check-ins keep our hearts young (certainly the level of discourse hovers around middle-school). But it also lightens our days. Keeps us focused on humor, upon which we agree. We are letting each other know, "I saw this goofy thing, I heard this goofy thing, this goofy thing happened to me...*and I thought of you*."

Still not gonna hug.

ROADWORTHY

The band was on a tight schedule to make load-in and soundcheck on the far side of the state, so we got an early start, the advantages of which evaporated ten minutes into the trip when the interstate shut down to a creep-and-crawl. This was especially frustrating as we were close to home and knew all the bypass shortcuts but the information was moot, trapped as we were bumper-to-bumper on the super slab.

I wish to report that we retired to the lounge area of the tour bus to pass the gridlock time but that is simply not true as we were five people, five guitars, one keyboard, one pedal steel, four amps, and various backpacks, suitcases, and cheese curds crammed in a Chevy van. Mostly we just sat there and talked. This ease in the face of a time crunch was a reflection of decades spent on the road; you'll make up the time somewhere, the speedometer is unaffected by your blood pressure, and things have a way of working out.

I never planned to be in a band. For starters, I can only play three chords on the guitar. OK, six, but only five on purpose. And as far as rhythm, well, I'm the guy who can't even polka. (And please don't write me notes about it being "just 1-2-3," because counting is not the problem here.) But some time ago I started writing songs as a hobby, then a buddy got me to sing some in a coffee shop, and now here we are rolling out over the open road like carefree diesel-fueled troubadours, our long hair flowing in the...

Well, that hasn't happened in years. In fact, as true rock-n-rollers we spent the first fifteen minutes of the traffic jam discussing per diem rates and self-employment taxes.

I've long wished I was more musically capable. That I'd had a garage band and paid my dues in taverns and could jam with the best of them. Instead I paid my dues as a typist, picked up songwriting on the side, wound up playing a few shows here and there with good musicians for nice people who like to listen, and then a few more shows, and a few still on the calendar, and you know what? That turned out pretty nice too because now instead of chasing our dreams down the neon highway we're just gonna drive a big chunk of Highway 10, pass the miles talking about ice fishing and dogs and urban planning and stop for gas, more cheese curds and beef sticks, and then drive some more, then find our way to the stage and lug our gear in and later lug it out, sing our songs in between, and drive that van half the night again just so we can wake up in our own beds, in a house with the people we love, and I guess we are chasing our dreams and may in fact have caught them, traffic jam on the interstate notwithstanding.

BIOSPHERE

After a record-breaking winter (in terms of snowfall, yes, but also in terms of ice dams, a leaking laundry room ceiling, and kerosene futures), we timed a family trip to Arizona imperfectly, departing Wisconsin the day spring finally arrived and crossing into the Grand Canyon State just as local temps hit 99 degrees. Having just weeks ago been up to my snoot in snowflakes for what seemed an epoch, I found this a particularly delicious hardship.

This being a brief family reunion trip we were resolved to spend time together no matter what. Our itinerary was fluid and driven by rumor, Post-Its, Google, backseat debate, and chance; so it was that on Day 2 we packed ourselves into a borrowed car and headed for the Santa Catalina Mountains and Biosphere 2.

My recollections of Biosphere 2 are based on—and impaired by—a smattering of vague references tied to the 1990s, a Pauly Shore movie I never saw, and something about people locked in a glass dome not getting along. I have since supplemented my insights with a Wikipedia skim, and in summary I am unequipped to mount an informed defense, criticism or general assessment of the place. I can only report that after a two-hour tour, our family felt it was worth the ticket.

I cannot speak for the others, but from my perspective, there were three elements to the visit I hope our children recall. The first was simply the wide range of oddities and interests within the whole works, from the R. Buckminster Fuller-inspired domes and latticework to the small gardening plots using olla (a small unglazed pot) irrigation methods to the gigantic "lungs" that equalize the pressure in the domes. To access the lungs we had to descend beneath Biosphere 2 to navigate a series of subterranean hallways and a sloped, steel-lined tunnel reminiscent of submarine innards. This expanded our sense of adventure.

The second element I appreciated was the presence of young folk and families. Not every face under the age of fifteen conveyed a waterpark or video game sense of joy and engagement, but you could see them looking and listening here and there, and whatever the scientific state of the structure, Biosphere 2 does implant the idea of intellectualism and academia as a source of adventure and betterment, and the subliminal message that in attempting to recreate the outside world inside we only deepen our appreciation for what an interconnected gift that outside world is.

Third, I emerged with a new respect for all the things I can learn from mistakes and failures and missteps when I am not consumed with pouncing on those errors as a way of validating my own cautious common sense. When I let go the easy story of nutty folks engaged in odd pursuits and focus instead on what might apply. The easy story is a way of letting myself off the hook. I am free to scoff and remain one half-inch above it all. It is the same with moonshots and electric cars and most everything new. Do some of the grander experiments deteriorate into failure and scientific soap operas? In many cases it would appear so. Is there anything to be learned from failures and soap operas? I reckon much of our world was built on same.

TINY HOUSE MARRIAGE ENCOUNTER

There's this woman I've been seeing off and on for the past 16 years, and last weekend I shacked up with her. Doesn't that sound exciting? In fact I've been married to her for 14 of those years. The "off and on" part speaks to our work and travel schedules as opposed to the relationship itself, which has been solidly "on" since we said "I do."

As any long-term pair can testify, "on" does not always mean "red-hot smooth auto-pilot love cruise," which is where the shack comes in. It's a smallish structure owned by friends in the northwoods. I was hiding out there in an attempt to hit some deadlines. The tiny house is remote and nestled amongst oaks, but does have electricity and cable TV in case you might want to pull a Walden but still catch the hockey playoffs.

I was set for a solo session when the weather changed. Snow, specifically, and what else would you expect in this our winter of busted records, shovel handles, and spirits? (Should you insist on noting it has "technically" been spring for over a month now, we will whack you with ice scrapers, roll you in our few remaining crumbs of rock salt, and bury you beneath the drift still visible on the far side of the pole barn.) This meteorology precipitated a cancellation that freed my wife from a previous commitment and she was able to join me for the weekend.

She brought work with her and we spent much of the time in separate spaces and separate endeavors. If that violates the Marriage Encounter Handbook, so goes self-employment. That said, we did sit face-to-face at a tiny table in the tiny house for meals and set aside a scheduled 1.5 hours each day for State of the Family discussions with an eye toward a Five Year Plan. Put that in a bouquet and lay it on your heart-shaped bedspread.

The concept of a Five Year Plan is rendered both essential and laughable in light of the State of Any Given Current School Morning, but if you can't impose your will on life you can at least nudge it, and putting things down on paper helps with context and reframing and momentum and priorities and now you're back at your Marriage Encounter. Privacy and respect prevent me over-divulging; let's just say there was at least one Ceremonial Sharing of Shortcomings Session, but we also worked on holding hands.

I take nothing for granted, least of all our marriage. I am a fool, but not that thick a fool. You do the work, you hope for the best, you remain open to change. And on the last night of the shack-up, you maybe skip the hockey and instead watch *When Harry Met Sally*, which is not our story, but contains plenty of lines that put you in a "compare and contrast" state of mind, not the worst exercise as you sit quietly on the couch beside someone going on your 17th year.

SPRING NOISE

It was noisy again out here in the countryside this morning. I say "again" because for the first time in months—though there still remains a strip of grainy snow along the base of the pole barn—temperatures have lifted to the point where we can raise our windows along with the mercury. After a hermetically sealed winter for the ages, in pours noise: the rat-a-tat of a woodpecker, a tractor churning through mud, chainsaws snarling across the valley, a proliferation of songbird whistle and chatter, poorly-mufflered pickup trucks running the county road down by the Zich place, boastful backyard roosters, the rattle of last year's oak leaves dropping through the branches after being displaced by this year's buds and then a breeze, and deep in the birches an unidentified bird whose one-note call I would describe as peevish (my ornithology is not up to snuff).

As tight as those windows were sealed all winter, as circumscribed as our wanderings were by snow banks, this spring has a special freshness despite it coming on slowly. The leaves aren't exactly busting out, but here and there they've extended an emerald fingernail, and we'll take it.

It is refreshing to be refreshed by the rediscovery of green, even in this my sixth decade of seasons. Between work and a family trip I spent a few weeks in the Arizona desert this winter, and yet I still managed to move more snow than I'd ever moved in my life. And that doesn't count all the snow my wife moved while I was gone and the plow truck broke. Twice.

I was as happy as a kid on the last day of school when I finally detached that plow from the truck last week. I felt light on my toes and so did the truck. If I never again have to don crampons to get the mail, or buy rock salt at a gas station, or scrape my windshield with a debit card, I doubt I'll miss it. I am prepared to suffer some snow-free Christmases within sight of sparkling saltwater. This winter triggered undeniable snowbird urges.

But: I am not yet not cured of the joy we feel as the land comes back to life. It's a classic Midwestern post-Calvinist guilt sorta thing, that in order to appreciate good times, we must first suffer hardship. That we must *earn* our sunburn, that we must wade through drifts before we wade through the surf, that we must slip on the ice before we drop it in lemonade.

This winter it took a front end loader and a whole lotta shoveling to keep a path clear to the chicken coop. Don't think I didn't appreciate it this morning when I walked out to do the chores and there was nothing but grass beneath my feet and sun upon my head. The forecast is for cloudy and cool. Spring's gonna duck behind the shed again for a few days. The asparagus will hesitate. But in the Norway pines behind the garage a robin was dive-bombing a red squirrel over nesting rights, adding to the noise declaring winter done.

INNER PEACE AND LEMMY

Insider note: This opening paragraph was a tongue-in-cheek passive-aggressive response to a reader who took me to task for the intentionally run-on closing paragraph of the "Roadworthy" essay a few pages back. I get my giggles where I can.

Perhaps the most unusual thing I can tell you about myself is that once during a German book tour for a book that didn't exist I not only presented a bilingual reading from the evaporated manuscript but sang a couple songs while strumming a warped, untuneable, and bedazzled acoustic guitar handed to me on the stage of an underground punk club in Frankfurt where the previous evening's guest artist had been Lemmy Kilmister, who some of you more ardent headbangers will recognize as the lead singer of the English heavy metal band Motörhead.

Well isn't that something, as my mother would say.

In fact, the preceding snippet of a synopsis doesn't begin to convey the convoluted weirdness of my one and only European book tour. It is a story to be told in chapters. Maybe some day.

We did get paid up front, so there's that.

I regret to inform you that in the time since I rocked Germany, Lemmy has—as one of his song titles would have it —been "Killed by Death," but his music lives on and will in fact bash your brains in. I cultivate a rustic and reflective image and just today I read three poems, attended a literary festival, and picked a tulip, but I am a cosmopolitan fellow, open to a wide range of cultural experiences, and when it comes to chores, Motörhead's cover of Metallica's "Whiplash" really helps pull the weeds, although before you crank the boom box you're going to want to make sure neither the vicar nor the children are within earshot. Certainly the chickens will be alarmed.

Lemmy is one of those folks of whom I like to say, "I'm glad he lived that way so I don't have to." You could say he was fully invested in his art, going to daily extremes to cultivate an image thematically consistent with the Motörhead's greatest hit, "Ace of Spades," a lullaby in the way a high-speed car crash is a drive in the country.

Lemmy's art required some real bad habits, which eventually caught up with him, although even as his health failed he kept at the bad habits with, as he said at the time, "dogged insolence in the face of mounting opposition to the contrary," and now you know he was a man of eloquence.

"I don't do regrets," said Lemmy as he approached the terminal off-ramp, and I can go along with that as long as we agree that *doing* regrets is not the same as *having* regrets. Because I have a prickly little passel of 'em, and while there's no use in wallowing, it doesn't hurt to revisit the hurt so we don't hurt again.

"Death is an inevitability, isn't it?" said Lemmy. "I don't worry about it. I'm ready for it. When I go, I want to go doing what I do best. If I died tomorrow, I couldn't complain. It's been good."

It has been good, Lemmy, and thank you for the reminder. Rest in noise. We'll always have Frankfurt.

PUFFED-UP PARTRIDGE

The temperature dropped as we were drove home through the cold rain, and the headlights caught the occasional snowflake. In the last light we saw the farm fields flooded all around us. Back home we had tilled the garden patches and set row markers but had done little more as everything was far too soaked for setting seeds or sprouts.

Earlier this week when it was sunny I drove my daughter to school and upon returning home found the driveway blocked by a male partridge soliciting companionship. His tail was fanned and the black feathers on his neck were flared in a cocky ruff. He wasn't strutting as such, but he was standing firm, slowly rotating and not about to budge for a used Toyota.

Drumming grouse are a signal sound of my childhood, and this spring as ever it is comforting to hear the airy, thumping crescendo of miniature sonic booms floating in from the aspen groves. There is always a sense of time travel, that I am the blue-jeaned kid on the back forty again, lazing through the woods on a Sunday afternoon, knowing school will be out in a few weeks and I can be Tom Sawyer all day long. Meanwhile I skulk through the underbrush trying to catch the booming bird in the act, but never do.

This driveway partridge—we never called them ruffed grouse—was in no position to drum, all flexed up as he was. I was happy to idle there and study him. Around here the turkeys run thick as rats on a dump and this time of year the toms are inflating themselves all over the place. It's rare to make the morning drive to school and back without seeing several of them holding court, sidle-circling each other in the corn fields and along the forest verge. But a partridge in full display is a much rarer sight.

There is something admirable in a bird that small fluffing himself up that big. I mean, sure, he is in the throes of all those throes nature infuses us with in order to maintain propagation of our respective species, and I trust his bravado was born more of desire than ferocity, but he didn't so much as fold a neck feather in deference to my presence. I found myself hoping there was a sweet lady partridge back there amongst the spruce and birches, cooing as he proved his love by facing down an all-wheel-drive steel machine.

In time I drove slowly forward. There were chores to be done, and a day to engage. The partridge tottered to the edge of the road, to where the first grass was greening up, then, after a final flex, folded his feathers and was suddenly a furtive little bird again, scooting through the barbwire and into the thicket.

Now we are returning home in the cold and dark and he's out there somewhere in it. Sometimes in winter ruffed grouse burrow into the snow, let it insulate and hide them. But by the time we pass his courting spot on the driveway the snowflakes are gone, replaced by straight wind-driven drizzle. I stick the car in the garage, grab a slicker and a flashlight, and lock down the chicken coop for the night. Come morning the fields will be further underwater. How grateful I am to climb the stairs and take to bed, the rain a patter against the shingles overhead.

APPLE BLOSSOMS

Yesterday a gust of wind hit the apple tree, filling the air with a flurry of white petals. It was a simultaneously beautiful and chilling sight. Beautiful because the petals were incandescent in the sunlight and fluttered to rest upon rich, green grass; chilling, because implicit in the vision was a message that already the blossoms were breaking up and before you know it we'll be pressing cider in anticipation of having something hot to drink after shoveling the mailbox free of real flurries.

Sometimes a guy gets a little ahead of himself.

To bring myself back to earth and diffuse the sense of speeding time, I headed down to the pole barn, where the implacable passage of days has once again clustered up the need for a thorough cleaning and probably a dumpster.

As long-time readers know, this isn't my first dumpster purge. I have also previously written of the electromagnetic nature of pole barns, how they draw objects of all sorts—ferrous and otherwise—to their center. You excavate, they re-accumulate.

But this time is different. Or so I silently swear. It's the same old dusty game of sort and toss, but lately I'm leaning heavily to toss. I'm at that age where I realize the percentage of things I've saved for a rainy day likely outnumber my remaining rainy days. There is also the irony of having just left the house after informing a child nothing fun will happen until she cleans her room only to be confronted by an entire buildings-worth of your own mess. And while it might be a piquant means of revenge, I cringe to think of my kids having to metaphorically pick up my room while literally sorting this hoard-o-rama for the auction.

In short I gotta get rid of a buncha stuff.

I put in a good couple of hours. Sorted out scrap metal, filled a box with recyclable wiring and electronics, chopped my "miscellaneous boards" pile into kindling. Sorted out plastics, refurbed a couple of old gas cans ("refurbed" being code for "Take that, non-spill nozzle!"), and threw all irredeemable materials into the dumpster pile. And—this is the critical part—time after time, I took a look at an object, enjoyed a memory or two, maybe snapped a photo with my phone, then dropped it into its proper category under the main heading: GOTTA GO.

When I signed off for the day and headed across the yard to help my wife in the garden, I still had a long ways to go. There remains a lot of dumpster crud to get through. If only a breeze would blow the pole barn clean as easily as it stripped those snowy white petals. That said, despite the wind, a thick fluff of blossoms still festoons the apple tree. Before I started the tiller I did—literally and in fact—stop to smell them. I do this knowing no season should be taken for granted. And should I be granted life and time to see these miniature blooms return, I pray the dumpster will not do the same.

TINY DANCERS

There were lawns to be mowed, but when you sign your youngster up for dance class you also sign yourself up for the culminating recital and so it was we found ourselves in a darkened auditorium on a sunny Sunday for a three-hour dance marathon.

The curtain rose on a row of giant flower pots, each planted with a tiny dancer in a tiny tutu. They were to bloom from the pots, and so they did, though not necessarily in the order or fashion intended, and the three dance coaches onstage were fully occupied in a combination of encouraging and herding. Of course the whole thing was darling and we the audience applauded accordingly as the flower pots and the last wandering dancer were cleared to make way for the next group.

The day's dancers ranged in age from preschool to high school seniors. Sometimes half the troupe was staring off into space. Sometimes there were six dancers and six different dances. And then there were the more accomplished performers, the ones who pirouetted beautifully, or flipped and flew above the stage as if gravity was optional, who hit their marks with crispness and grace.

I'll say this: The dance company kept things moving. One after the other the ensembles ran to their places, struck their poses, and waited for the lights and music. What happened next varied widely depending on age and skill level, but rarely did we wait.

And they just kept coming. When intermission finally arrived, I texted a fellow father whose child was enrolled in lessons with another dance company. "Halfway through a three-hour dance recital," I typed. "Pray for me."

I regretted the joke immediately. Because truth was, I didn't really mean it. I wasn't the least bit bored. Even though our daughter danced with the third group out, we remained engaged throughout. It was easy, really, what with all the life and innocent beauty on display. Children dancing—some without regard for choreography or rhythm, a few transfixed into immobility by the lights, now and then one scooting to the front of the stage to wave and look for grandma—are the personification of hope. To watch them run eagerly to the stage, to be utterly absorbed by the music and the moment, was to see them exploring the possibility that magic can be found in movement. That even if the dance is not graceful, there is grace in the attempt.

And the upshot for us grownups is we can't help but remember what it was to move simply through joy, without concern for what others might think (although it helps if you're decked in sequins). And it is difficult to obsess over the electric bill or how you oughta be home mowing the lawn when a teenaged ballet dancer knocks out six perfect spins, or a child decorated like a daisy finally emerges from her flower pot and leaps about the stage in random happiness, never mind the beat.

Yes, the lawn went unmowed. But as reward for those three hours gone, we emerged to a world where it seemed the sun shone all the brighter.

HOMEBOUND VAN

The big rain hit right as we rounded Rib Mountain. It was pelting real heavy while we carved the concrete skyway in a leftward curve to home, then when we got pointed straight west it thinned to a spatter and finally just a spritz now and again. Meanwhile the wind had got up in a relentless bluster, and was bossing the old van around. It wasn't handling well in the first place, so jammed with music gear and merchandise and musicians that it was squatting in the hind end and tending to "waller," as the phrase of my people has it. Full attention forward, two hands on the wheel, hammer down for Thorp.

The lead guitar player had been fiddling around with the radio, and when he dozed off in the passenger seat, it was tuned to a country oldies station. The pedal steel player was out cold one row back amidst a heap of backpacks, merch boxes, hard cases and our special hand-crank coffee grinder for use in hotel coffee emergency situations. The bass and banjo players had taken a separate vehicle. That left me the only one present and conscious, so I focused on the road and sang along with every hit that radio fed me. One of the glories of a good country song is you can be driving an over-loaded Toyota past dairy barns in central Wisconsin singing along with George Strait to "Amarillo by Morning" and fully inhabit the idea of rollin' a diesel doolie and a horse trailer hitch to one more rodeo.

It's been a rich life and I'm not sure I deserve it, but these are some of my favorite moments. Just the low-level workaday business of going about our business, taking our little show on the road and back home. Tomorrow my elder daughter is leaving for college. An introductory summer course, but she'll be crossing over to another state and certainly another stage. I want to be home to see her off.

I just kept singing along to those old songs and fighting the wind. Somewhere around Stanley the guitar player woke up, and then the steel player, and just in time, too, because the sun was laying a molten bead along the edges of the sky-sliding clouds and it was something to see, the grays and whites and purples all afire to the west, and then to the south-east a series of rainbows, appearing and disappearing for the final stretch.

Right as we curled around the 29 off-ramp and south on 53 to our homes, the oldies station served up Suzy Bogguss and her 1992 hit, "Letting Go." You got a daughter headed off to college, that's a sweet whomper of a number. I kept it together but there were home movies playing in my heart.

The van odometer is about to hit 222,222 miles. We thought we might make it on this trip and were ready with our phone cameras but our math was off and it didn't happen. It'll probably click over this week during a mundane trip to the post office. By then I will have waved my daughter out the driveway. Right now she is in her room asleep. I leave the van to cool in the garage and stare at her darkened window, grateful to be home, grateful to sleep one more night beneath the same shingles.

CHICKEN IN THE NIGHT

I woke to poultry screeching in the night. "I thought I heard a chicken," I told my wife in the dark. "I think it *was* a chicken," she said, sounding shaken. The tremble in her tone was due less to the sound of the freaked-out bird than my having lurched from snoring slug to street-fighting sheet-flinger in a split second. Last week when a midnight backyard lightning strike dropped thunder that rattled the house to its bones and raised the entire family, I slumbered like a baby in a bassinette. And yet other triggers—the sound of fire pagers, a baby's whimper, late-arriving teenagers, and chickens under assault—galvanize me. I don't so much wake as erupt.

This sounded as if it were directly below our bedroom window. Which made no sense, since all of our chickens were tucked safely in the coop clear over by the granary. I had locked them down myself before coming in for the night.

Just as suddenly as I kipped off the mattress the chicken had gone silent. In fact I was already questioning if I had heard it at all. It was already becoming dreamlike. I dropped my head to the pillow and was out again. I once awoke in a tent in Budapest to feel a thief kneeling on my feet and rummaging in my backpack. It was pitch black so I just rared up and punched the darkness with everything I had. My knuckles smacked a face, I heard a body tumble backward, I heard feet running away in the night. And I went right back to sleep. My wife suffers from insomnia and is displeased that neither thunder nor thieves nor squalling birds prevent my dropping off to dreamland in a trice.

At dawn it occurred to me that I couldn't recall seeing one of our favorite hens lately. It was possible that I'd have overlooked her in the flock, but she was bright and distinctive and usually first to the feeder, and she hadn't been leading the charge down the ramp lately. Also, a week ago when we were working in the garden, she appeared out of nowhere and from the direction of our deck rather than the coop, where all the other chickens were fenced in. At the time I had written it off to her intelligence, small size, and propensity for finding even the smallest gap in the netting. But now I realized she might have been nesting and not returning to the coop at night.

Sure enough, down around behind the deck at the base of the lilac tree, I discovered a clutch of eggs. Two of them were broken. Worse, I saw a scatter of feathers in the hen's distinctive pattern. They trailed out of the weeds and across the yard.

So it was no dream, it was a varmint. Maybe a coon, maybe a fox, perhaps a fisher. One sweet little chicken, gone in the night. I have no snappy wrap-up. Sometimes that sound in the night is exactly what you fear. And by the time you hear it, there is nothing to be done. Over on the hutch there is a catalog. You can order chickens and they arrive peeping in the U.S. Mail. In times of darkness we appreciate little miracles.

VULNERABILITY

Over the course of the past month, I have participated in several conversations—largely independent of each other and across a range of folks including a life coach in Colorado, a Grammy-winning musician, various friendly strangers, and my wife—in which the common denominator was the word *vulnerability*.

I first began giving regular consideration to the power of vulnerability while reading the work of my old dead friend Michel de Montaigne, the French essayist and philosopher for whom my main affection arises from him predicating his entire oeuvre on the idea that "I could be wrong." In this our age of bellicose certitude, admitting you might be wrong is to show your soft underbelly, even as the snark army sharpens its ideological knives.

In the case of the musician, he and I were in the small room above my garage revisiting those times when we'd offered something from the heart, only to have it kicked to the gutter like desiccated dog waste. Harsh words and one-star reviews are not bullets, but they will send you ducking for cover. I have more than once curled up to suck my figurative thumb.

The musician and I hardly expect our every utterance to be greeted with unanimous hosannas. We know ourselves, our audiences, and the world itself better than that. Nor is our work always worthy. It's just that sincerity is a form of vulnerability, and you never quite get over being the kid who shows up with a homemade birthday present only to be teased for its imperfections.

Lately whenever I mention the word vulnerability people bring up Brené Brown, who has attracted a large following for her research, writing, and presentations on the subject. The second or third time I heard her name I got a little whiny, as one will when one you think you've been thinking something up yourself only to find someone far more educated and eloquent than you has been on the job for years... and also maybe she sells a lot more books than you. Good news is, admitting I can be this petty leaves me vulnerable to critiques of selfishness and self-centeredness, which in turn helps me look deeper into the more dimly-lit corners of my mirror. Also, I am typing this from the passenger seat on I-35 en route to a family event in Wichita while listening to Brené Brown's latest audiobook, so I am not all that put out.

The musician and I spoke a good long while. To be clear, this was not some ponderous pensivity panel. We also discussed the specifics of self-employment as it relates to used vans, how my chickens were doing, how our true friends keep us alive and in line, and he handed over a couple bags of high-end coffee beans. Ultimately, the musician and I agreed vulnerability is essential to goodness. Tell your story, share your heart. The slings and arrows will come. But so will the ones who understand. The fellow travelers. And together you'll travel toward one thing: Gratitude.

FIREFLIES AGAIN

Today's question: how does one *not* write about the fireflies?

I saw the first blue-green wink two weeks ago but had forsworn reporting on the topic as I have written about the brilliant bugs so many times in the past. Then last night after a long walk out back I climbed out of the valley to the ridge and turned for home in the gloaming only to find myself treading a tunnel of twinkles.

This pure visual delight gave me something to ponder as I stumped the final half mile to the yard. How we might see something for the thousandth time and yet see it for the first time one more time. Those bugs are really something.

I set off on this stroll in part because I hadn't hardly moved my lard over the course of the day, but also because I had spent far too much of the day staring at electrons, which as we know are negatively charged. To wrap the day wading through a hidden holler of overgrown goldenrod seemed just the thing.

Some of the electrons I scanned comprised an article detailing the spread of ticks and their associated diseases throughout the United States. The term "pandemic" was invoked (I'm never clear on the definition of that one, apart from, "No thank you."). The country boy in me wants to scoff at tick warnings as softie silliness, as I was raised on the phrase "tick check" and we made sport of squashing the fat ones on the barn floor, but it is clear things have taken a turn. Several of our family members have had Lyme. In some cases the effects have reverberated for years. Now there are other strains of tick, and other strains of trouble. Before setting out on my walk I sprayed the cuffs of my jeans with repellent then spritzed the other exposed bits of me with good old-fashioned "Off!" There are more organic options available in the house but in my experience the insects treat them as salad dressing.

So the tick hordes are en route. I guess it's just one more wave in a tide of unease seeping through the national consciousness. We are constantly riding a wobble-board teetering between hunkering down and throwing up our hands. Or stepping off the board and covering our eyes, hoping it makes us invisible. Lately I have found some relief in quietly supporting the efforts of other people smarter than me. More *effective* than me. People who subscribe to a blend of thoughtful reflection ruddered by practicality and pragmatism.

As a father I chew daily on how best to prepare my children for the future we are giving them. Short on solutions, I tend to focus more on navigation skills. Among these I intend to recommend technology-free hikes that end in darkness broken by intermittent stipples of bioluminescence, just the sort of thing to ease your mind before you shut the chickens in and get some rest before whatever tomorrow brings.

GARDENING

Ginny down in the valley brought us a fat bag of asparagus. Ginny's an expert gardener with decades of experience in the professional plant business. She's retired now, but her vegetable garden remains a showcase. You could shoot seed catalog photos amongst the rows. Please note if you want to track down Ginny and ask for her definition of "retired," first put on your running shoes.

As for our family, we've been on a gardening hiatus the last couple of years, raising nothing but garlic and asparagus. This year—partly because we were outside one night, the weather was beautiful, and our hearts were silly with delusion—we dove back in. I put the tiller on the tractor and churned up a vast plot. Our new neighbor Kent came over to help so we could get in way over our heads extra fast. We tried an earth-friendly experiment in which rather than plastic we lined the rows with butcher paper weighted down with bricks. We raked and smoothed and mounded and hilled and tilled, and then we planted carrots, basil, beans, cucumber, onions, sunflowers, potatoes, kale, lettuces, chard, watermelon, squash, and whatever else we had rattling around in the seed packets we found on the porch. In the last light, we stood uphill and gazed upon the gentle land, fragrant with tilling.

That night it rained. Hard, and with wind. The butcher paper that didn't disintegrate tore loose and laid itself across the hillside like brown windrows. Then it rained some more. And got cold. And stayed cold. And rained some more. Eventually some beans sprouted. The onion sets peeked out but tentatively so. The kale popped forth, then didn't get any bigger for two weeks. I feared the potatoes had gone rotten in the ground, but eventually they too emerged, although slowly, more in caution than abundance.

There were vast patches that germinated not at all.

The weeds? They blew up like a Henri Rousseau jungle painting. At one point we waded through them, putting down little surveyor's flags wherever we recognized a plant we actually hoped to harvest. Then I fetched the lawn mower and did the weeding.

Now we've had a good run of sun. I've hilled the potatoes a couple of times and they're leafing up a hefty green. The carrots, squash and cucumbers are spotty but coming on. The tomatoes are profuse and the basil is keeping pace. The garlic looks great. If nothing else we'll soon have bruschetta. And organic comfort foods come winter.

For now, we're enjoying Ginny's asparagus. Ours has been an utter flop. A few measly spears. You coulda wrapped one hand around the entire bunch. We're not sure what went wrong. Ginny says her asparagus is misrepresentative, and the rest of her garden isn't doing so well. I'll believe it when I see it. If her definition of a poorly garden is anything like her definition of retirement, good luck keeping up. That first night we grilled the spears and served them simply: drizzled with olive oil, dusted with salt. On plate and palate, a neighbor's gift of peace and plenty. So simple, so enough.

THE BUG IS BACK

Once upon a time in Germany my grandfather bought a brand-new 1967 Volkswagen Beetle straight off the lot. After using the car to tour its country of origin, he packed it on a cargo ship, then flew home to America. The details are lost to history, but at some point the ship sailed into a U.S. port, the Beetle debarked, and Grandpa drove it home to Eau Claire, Wisconsin.

I retain vague memories of riding in the bug with Grandma. I remember our fascination with the motor being in the rear and the trunk in the front. The sewing-machine sound of it compared to the big Chevies and roaring Fords we were used to. The rounded eave overhanging the license plate. Its petite chromed and twinned tailpipes. The unfamiliar seatbelt clips. The slot behind the seat where Grandma stored her knitting bag.

Over time the Beetle was sidelined for more modern vehicles. For cars that zoomed faster and had more room and didn't subject the driver to frostbitten toes during the Wisconsin winters. It'd get driven now and then, and Grandpa lent it out to family. My brother John remembers taking it musky fishing. He must have had to break the rod down to get it in there. I don't know the whole story (that'd take a family reunion), but eventually it wound up parked alongside my sister's garage up north. "I'm gonna get it goin' again," said my brother-in-law Mark fifteen years ago, when he was helping me resurrect my 1951 International Harvester pickup in that same garage.

Last weekend we were gathered at a party up the road from the home farm to celebrate a neighbor's 80th birthday when Mark and my sister Kathleen came rolling up the gravel road in what's left of that Volkswagen.

It turns out the Beetle was rusted beyond rescue. Road salt and moldering time are to blame, but when he started deconstructing it, Mark also discovered rust deposits in odd spots including the interior of the window posts. A former Navy man, he theorizes the oxidation was hastened by the time the car spent in the salt air. And so, in a process that cannot be done justice in the space of this column but says a lot about why you will want them on your side for the apocalypse, Mark, Kathleen, and their son took a torch to the VW, remounted it atop a junked-out and jacked-up four-wheel-drive Suzuki Samurai, painted it flat green with black trim, fitted it with an exteriorized wrap-around roll cage, and, well, if you are directing the next *Mad Max* sequel, you need to get them on the horn right now.

A bunch of us took rides in the thing, including my daughter who loves cats and bamboo straws and musicals but also—based on the width of her grin—four-wheel-drive monster bugs. Apart from the hood ornament, steering wheel button, instrument panel, and recognizable silhouette, there's not a lot of the old VW left. The dashboard remains its original red, and Mark wants to repaint it but Kathleen says let it be.

I took my turn at the wheel, navigating a dirt two-track

through the pines. As we rumbled along on four big fat rubber luggers, it was nice to glance at the gleaming red dash and imagine Grandpa tooling around Europe five decades ago, putting the first kilometers on a story still rolling up the miles.

Postscript: When Mark registered the "new" vehicle, it took a long time. The original documents were written in German, and the new documents had to incorporate the Suzuki. "I'd keep them both in the glove compartment," said the woman at the DMV.

TALENT CONTEST

Art can be harder than you think, especially if you are a ballet dancer competing with pig races.

I came to this conclusion while sitting with the audience observing the semifinals of our regional state fair talent contest. A high school girl had just finished singing a gentle ballad, competing all the while with an unseen but thumpingly present marching band playing a tune conducted in a conflicting tempo and key. Go ahead and try that next time you're at a parade. It's the sonic equivalent of rubbing your belly while patting your head with a bass drum mallet.

Taking the stage before strangers is tough enough. When the majority of those strangers are milling about in search of cheese curds, cotton candy, and prize rutabagas against a soundscape of ring-a-ding attractions, carnival barkers, screeching carnival rides and riders, distant livestock calls, and a P.A. announcer paging lost parents, well, then, supreme focus on the part of the performer is required. The landing pad for the helicopter rides is right across the lot, and every tour begins with the chopper blasting an arc above the tree-line behind the stage. Contestants were warned ahead of time to ignore it and power through; no do-overs for flyovers.

The participants performed with composure beyond their years, soldiering on despite all distractions. For the singers it's great preparation for those times when they find themselves serenading a bar filled with hooting bachelor party bros, or at an outdoor gig beneath a tent adjacent an airbase. For the dancers it's good preparation for...well, I don't know, but they'll be prepared. And to see young people gracefully unspooling ballet as the guy two doors down does Johnny Cash covers and half the front row is eating deep-fried pickles, well that's art happening right where it oughta happen.

Unavoidably, talent contests come with built-in heartbreak. Especially for the twelve-and-unders. In some cases these are children opening their hearts to the world for the first time. One young man wept openly after the results were announced. I went over and shook his hand, told him how grateful I was that he got up there and sang that song. And that he didn't just sing but that he worked up his own dance steps. I told him I hope he keeps performing. Have you ever tried to convey something so strongly it hurt your heart?

One of my offspring entered this year's contest. Ahead of time we discussed all the angles: give it your all so no matter how it goes you won't have the regret of holding back, be gracious, be grateful, know that it won't always be your day. Do your best, then whichever way it goes, *be* your best. Things didn't pan out the way she hoped. She got to practice the essential, difficult art of poise in disappointment. But what you've got there is Life 101, the short course.

And then, because—win or otherwise—we are committed to her broad education in the arts, we crossed the midway, ascended the grandstand and took in a 90-minute class on how to hang in there for the long haul delivered in musical form by Professor Joan Jett.

PICKING BERRIES

Headlines and deadlines having dumped me in a brackish stew, I decided it was time to take some sun. I left my air-conditioned room above the garage, grabbed a plastic tub from a drawer in the kitchen, and headed out to pick black caps. Everywhere I looked they were thick on the bush.

I started out alongside the driveway, where the brambles intertwine with grapevine, which in turn has woven itself in and around the sagging barbwire strung to contain cows absent this farm for thirty years now. I wonder what it was like when the ground on the other side of the fence was well-grazed, back in the days before the barn burned, when the milk truck rumbled out of here filled with its sloshing, frothy gallons. Back when 30-40 Holsteins was considered big-time. The smoke was still clearing when the farmer asked his sons if any of them planned to follow in his footsteps. Nope, they said, and so they dozed the whole smoldering works into a hole and that was that.

The first berries dropped *tap-tap* into the tub. I had no plans to make jam or put up preserves. Apart from a row of raspberries and some blueberry bushes, we don't have a berry patch as such; they just grow hither and yon in the woods and along the fencelines. Every year we try to gather some—and some remnant orchard apples—more as an acknowledgement than a harvest. I figured to pick a few dozen, eat them, give the gods a nod, and get back to work.

But about forty berries in I decided to just keep going. I needed the rhythm of the reach and pluck. Needed to feel the sun warm my neck. Needed to drain my brain of rancidity. Berry-picking seemed just the thing.

It was a perfect afternoon. The air was thick with bird-song. The breeze was whisper-soft. Just enough to clear the bugs. The entire picking session, I slapped two mosquitos. No gnats, no deer flies. Every tree was at peak green, the living definition of lush. All around were leaves steeped in sun, photosynthesis in the flesh.

I picked and let my mind go where it would. Reached down in there deep, where the fresher canes glowed pale green. Focused on the delicate pinch of pulling the berry without squishing it. Now and then a nettle or a thorn, just nip and scratch enough to heighten the moment. A little habanero in the soup. An hour passed, the container was brimming and heavy in my hand, and my mind was clear.

I topped the black caps with two dozen raspberries from the patch that has otherwise mostly failed this year, and passed over the blueberries, still a dusty green. Swung down by where that barn used to stand and picked a final handful just for me. Ate them on the spot, then placed the tub on the kitchen island where the rest of the family would find it when they returned home.

Returning to my room above the garage, I read Wendell Berry's "The Peace of Wild Things," and got back to work.

GREG BROWN (ONE MORE TIME)

I once interviewed the singer Greg Brown on a park bench in Iowa City. For the first few minutes I was distracted by an intermittent subterranean vibration passing through the bench similar to those generated by subway cars in New York City. There had been a lot of changes in Iowa City but I was pretty sure they hadn't installed a subway. Then I noticed the vibrations commenced whenever Greg Brown spoke, and ceased when he went silent.

I once wrote that Greg Brown's voice "*sounds as if it was aged in a whiskey cask, cured in an Ozarks smokehouse, dropped down a stone well, pulled out damp, and kept moist in the palm of a wicked woman's hand. I think if he says good morning across his coffee cup, it raises ripples. The voice is a perfect match to his lyrics, biblical and bar stool and garden loamy as they are, all Rexrothian and as easy-rolling true as a brand-new '64 Dodge.*"

That voice was center-stage beneath the Lake Superior Big Top Chautauqua tent up there by Bayfield last week as Greg Brown gave the final show of his touring career. He appeared at a benefit a week later and has plans for a scattering of similar events, but as far as packing up his guitar and fishing rod to hit the calendar-driven circuit as he has for decades, he's says that's over.

Greg Brown is one of those artists who helped me understand you could care about literature and art and beauty and poetry and still love dirt and fishing and Slant Six engines. That it was just fine to listen to Dylan Thomas Caedmon recordings in an old pickup truck. First time I heard him sing *"I'm a Midwest boy, I'm a big dumb man,"* I thought, *Yep*. It is also relevant that the first show I ever saw at Lake Superior Big Top Chautauqua was a Greg Brown concert, an evening of music that led directly to me—this very week—celebrating my 15th wedding anniversary.

A year after I interviewed Greg Brown on that park bench I went on a book tour that took me through Kansas City. I dropped by Rainy Day Books to sign their stock. There was no audience, just me at the counter writing my name. Glancing to my left I saw a guy reading Dostoevsky. *That looks like Greg Brown*, I thought. I wasn't going to bother him, but right then he looked up, made eye contact, and said, "Dude." He recognized me from Iowa City. We conversed briefly. I kept my cool, but inside it was a fan-boy moment, and back in the car I thought, *He remembered me!* Then I looked down and realized I was wearing the exact same pants, boots and T-shirt as I had that day on the park bench.

Backstage at the Big Top after his final show, we shot the breeze. Mostly about poetry and raising daughters. We relived the Rainy Day Books moment, and he says he would have recognized me even if I had changed clothes. As far as Mr. Brown's retirement, I don't have any red-hot scoop other than he's 70 now and feels it's time. I figure that's good news for his garden, to which he may now tend after leaving us a lifetime of musical preserves.

CUCUMBERS

I was caught off guard when the cucumber leaves fell in a wilt. Spring and summer have been rain-gauge busters, the basement is persistently squishy, and the down-valley corn-fields are stunted and pocked with freshborn ponds. So this little spot of drought was slow to register. All that precipitation, then it only took a few days for half the garden to go hardpan.

As regular readers of this column already know, my use of the word "garden" is an oversell be it invoked as either noun or verb. But by recent experience I can tell you that even a poor garden is a garden. We've put up a dozen jars of pesto and already the basil is bushed out again. There are vast racks of garlic drying in the barn. The squash patch is weedy but when I part the foxtail and lambsquarter to peek through there are acorns and butternuts fattening on the ground. The eggplants are royal, bulbous, and magnificent, and the last time I passed through the kitchen I spied baba ganoush in process.

And my favorite—backyard bruschetta—is well in season

and supply. To step out the door and gather up the ingredients an hour or so before you intend to eat them, tear the basil, chop the garlic, slice the onion paper thin, dice the tomatoes, fiddle with the ratio of balsamic vinegar and olive oil, let the whole works mull on the counter so the flavors can intermingle, only stirring in the cheese as the bread slices toast...the results will make you gardener of the year if only in your own mind and belly.

There are other happy surprises. In spite of our neglect the kale is hale. We've had a limited but hearty selection of carrots. And despite a persistence of potato bugs it appears we'll have all the baked, boiled and mashed we can handle.

On the flip side, most of our lettuce was subsumed by thickets of inedible greens. Rabbits got a swath of the chard, deer got to the beans, and we have watermelon vines but no melons. The sweet corn never even sprouted.

And yet we can revel in the taste of something fresh. Last week, prior to the cucumbers wilting, our elder daughter returned from an extended trip away from home. The girl loves pickles and vinegar, so around noon I went to the garden and picked a batch of cucumbers, an onion, and some dill. After slicing the cucumbers and onion, I doused them in vinegar, seasoned them with the dill and fresh-ground pepper, and left them to marinate in a tureen. The look on her face that evening when she stepped through the door and spotted the bowl was almost enough to convince me to tackle her college aid form again. She pulled up a chair and tucked in, making happy little noises that didn't sound like a teenager at all. Sometimes I get the Dad thing right.

Last night a decent rain fell. A soaker, as opposed to the more recently common gully-cutters. This morning the cucumber leaves were flush and flared. We are out of the running for Garden of the Year, but I just heard a man on an economics podcast declare it was time to "establish a more robust value proposition," and now that the cukes are back, I'd say we're there.

PLUM EFFECT

This year my wife and I pruned the little plum tree out there by the swing set. Before we started cutting, we viewed several instructional videos. It's terrific to live in an age where all this information is available on a pocket-sized touch screen so that you can stand there with your neck bent for forty-five minutes and really study things out until you're deeply and professionally confused. In this our digital information age, the phrase "experts agree" has really taken a hit.

Eventually we weighed all our options, split the difference and commenced to snipping and chopping. I worried we'd been over-severe, but soon the tree leafed out thick and full. Furthermore, the arboreal haircut had a bonsai effect; the tree appeared more artful against the horizon (once we repositioned the chicken coop).

Just one problem: Last year, in an untrimmed state, the tree was loaded with fruit. This year, the yield is down by over half.

Off and on over the summer, I've wondered: Did we prune incorrectly? Over-aggressively? A week too soon or late? Did we somehow sicken rather than strengthen the tree?

Did we introduced something that sapped the sap? I'm sure the experts will weigh in, although based on all those pruning videos, I fear my current schedule will not support the weight of wading through all the weighing.

Last week, I gave the tree closer inspection. The plums in place were plump. No problem there. But they were definitely scarce on the limb. I was still at a loss as to what we had done wrong.

Then we rented a dumpster. Seems unrelated, until I tell you it was to clean out the pole barn (again) and down beside the pole barn there is a giant unconstrained natural-born plum tree that towers and splays every whichway and has never been pruned in its life. Last year it was positively laden with fruit. But this year, as I chonked yet another box of mice-nibbled keepsakes into the garbage scow, I noticed something: The overgrown plum tree has some nice plums, but they are hit-and-miss.

I spent the rest of the day pondering what I shall write up in all the journals as The One Plum Tree Effect. That is to say, what conclusions might I have carried all the rest of my life had I not looked at the unpruned tree? How many times would I have told the story about how us trimming the first tree knocked the plums out of it? When—based on my sample study of two different trees—it turns out it mighta just been the weather. Or some bug I can't see.

Not being Aesop, I'm not sure how to wrap this up. I'm sure there's something in here about confirmation bias, or causation versus correlation, or blah-di-blah. For now I'm working the idea that the plum trees seem to be telling me to beware first impressions formed through faulty interpretations. That firsthand observation can still lead to a false narrative. That between those two trees we're still gonna get some jam.

MONARCHS

Having been holed up beneath a roof all the cloudy morning, when the sun broke through I took a turn around the yard and garden. Right off the office steps I got flutter-swooped by a Monarch butterfly. Once when we were children on the farm we woke to find the white pine in our yard saturated with Monarchs in migration. It was a wonder with staying power. I hold it in memory as a miracle.

Next, while running mundane errands I heard a radio advertisement for a plastic surgeon purveying multiple means of trimming, tucking, and smoothing pretty much everything but your toenails. Fair enough, and here at half-past fifty the images in my bathroom mirror have fostered compassion in my heart for those who do seek certain resets. The radio spot concluded with a declaration that submitting to this surgeon's rejuvenating tools would render me "younger and more relevant."

I drove a good half block before that word *relevant* regis-tered. They just kinda laid it in there smooth-like and I skated right over it. But jeepers: *Relevant?* As leverage goes, that's a little hinky. A few hours later I was still turning it over in my head. I couldn't quite figure why it was working me like a sand grain in my shoe. Among the factors impairing my relevance, I figure a loosening jawline doesn't even make the top fifty. And yet still I was bugged. Then I saw my daughter skip across the yard and I imagined her hearing that a surgical do-over was the key to relevance. Or her well-lined and well-loved *grandmother* being told the same. I found myself toying with the idea of scheduling an appointment just to give the surgeon an opportunity to expand on this line of thinking.

Then late last night I got into one of those earworm-wormhole situations involving YouTube algorithms and old country music. Wound up watching Don Williams videos and missing my daughter's great-grandma, a Bible-studying woman of rectitude who believed Mr. Williams was the best country singer ever. Eventually Don Williams ran out and I was served up Willie Nelson singing "It Gets Easier," then Willie Nelson singing "Blue Eyes Cryin' In The Rain," accompanied by his adult sons. These are recent Willie. Singing from a chair, not a stage. On "Blue Eyes" he looks frail, content, and centered. His face is a worn leather treasure map, as was Grandma's by the end. Who would yank the wrinkles out of either and consider it a victory for relevance?

As have many folks of late, we have taken to leaving our milkweed patches to thrive in hopes of bolstering the Monarch population in face of recent declines. Based strictly on observation, Sunday dinner conversation up north, and last Thursday's debriefing conducted roadside over the recycling bins with my neighbor Denny, general consensus has it this is a good year for Monarchs. I hope so. I have also noted honeybees in our sunflowers, so hang in there, apiarists.

Reconstruction can be resurrection. Even if it's something

short of that I have no quibble, and in short, it's none of my beeswax. But *relevant*? Let's reserve that for the real deal, in this case my daughter, hand in my hand, our faces to the sun as the butterflies rise.

THE RHYME

The last windstorm took down a major branch of our big apple tree. It hasn't been pruned in over a decade, so Mother Nature did the job herself. What's handy is, the branch snapped only partially through, then draped gently to the ground, meaning the leaves remain green and the entire bough of fruit is in reach. You can just walk up and select an apple in the vertical.

This week I spoke with a man on an island who said the course of history is cyclical, each rotation activated when a confluence of events triggers a cosmic reset button. History does not repeat itself, the man said, nor does it simply rhyme; rather, it rhymes in reverse. I'll have to chew on that a while before I can digest it. If his theory strikes you as hoo-hah, I should add he has made millions putting his money where his theory is, and while the term "reset button" was his own, I'm the one who stuck "cosmic" in there.

I have gotten to where I'm at today thanks in part to my sense of cosmic poetics. This has filled my life with richness if not riches. As predilections go, a poetic bent has its pros and cons. Many are the times I wish I could just fix a carburetor, or hang a door straight, or make a million being crass on Instagram. Instead I settle for a sputtering weed-whacker, rhyming things on the page if not in reality, and—when the rhyming pays off—putting a little something into a middle-of-the-road mutual fund. Some of us are market-timers. Some of us are pluggers. Either way we're gambling on the length of the cycle.

It's been one of those workaday weeks. Paid the bills but didn't get the checkbook balanced. Read the news, then decided not to read the news. Got some wood put up toward winter, but not enough for the whole winter. Hit some deadlines, begged off on some others. Doled out advice to my daughters then turned right around and sought advice from my friends. Said the right thing, said the wrong thing, eventually said what needed to be said. Showed up where I needed to show up when I needed to show up, but never with time to spare. Seven days straight just working at it, then broke a little bit to the good side of even. What you got there is a win if not a million.

My buddy Mills has a homemade meat smoker. He says he'll come cut up that apple branch after the leaves drop. Do me some venison strips in trade. That's a nice rhyme. Easier to find than the reverse rhyme, at the right time. Maybe the key to cutting through to clarity is kicking loose the soft hobble of poetics. But not today. Rather I'll plug away, maybe take a break and ease over across the yard, grab an eye-level apple, that first sweet bite a reset button sufficient for the moment.

PAEAN

Up in Bayfield this week the green was going thin on the leaves and there were patches of blaze. It is tempting to continue in this vein and compose a paean to autumn, but I've likely overplayed that tune, you know how it goes, and also *paean* is a tricky word, as I found out earlier this year when I included it in an essay which I read aloud for the very first time in front of a conference room filled with librarians, a notoriously well-read bunch.

As I assume most of you do when reading aloud, my eyes were scanning four or five words ahead of my mouth. I was probably half a second out from paean when I spotted it lying in wait and realized I knew how to spell it, I knew what it meant, but I had no idea how to pronounce it. Time slowed down in my head as I ran through all the possibilities. As it turns out you can pop up a pretty good head sweat in half a second. In the end I marble-mouthed it, in the hopes the audience might assume the microphone wasn't up to snuff. I guess you could call it a glossal gloss-over.

Paean is a lovely word by definition (song of praise or triumph) as well as on the page. I'm a sucker for words in which vowels nestle adjacent. *Aesthetic*, for example, which I prefer over *esthetic* (which, in the end, is what (a)esthetics is all about). You put an a next to an e, they look round and gentle and friendly. Pleasant to observe.

But sometimes a little harder to pronounce.

After my talk I had other duties, so it wasn't until I got back in the van for the drive home that I had time to look up the pronunciation on my phone. As it turned out, as well as paean works on the page, it really isn't suited for reading aloud, as it is pronounced "pēən" which sounds a lot like something you shouldn't be doing in public and isn't all that aesthetic no matter how you spell it. Turns out marble-mouthing was the right move.

In the interest of personal character and full disclosure and in spite of what I thought at the time, in the course of looking up the pronunciation, I discovered I actually *didn't* know how to spell paean. I had been going with *paen*. This triggered another crop of head-sweat and a quick call to the editor of a certain national online publication where the essay was already live and garnering hundreds of hits. Thankfully, it appears no one else knew how to spell it either, and we got it fixed before any of your topflight spellers blasted the comments section.

So your correctly spelt paean contains a triple-vowel-nestle. This is soothing to look upon, even this morning as the temperatures hit the low fifties, upshot being today I will forgo autumnal songs of praise and triumph and instead compose another stack of firewood.

BONFIRE STORIES

Last night a man showed me a photo of his parents taken around the time they met. His father was a midwestern G.I. stationed overseas, his mother a Japanese seamstress. Faced with a language barrier and no other means of arranging a date, the young soldier would purposely cut the buttons from his uniform so he had an excuse to visit the seamstress.

Decades evaporate. The soldier and the seamstress are gone, the black-and-white photos taken when they met paired with a snapshot of the two of them gray-haired and elderly, framed and smiling from the wall of a small rural Wisconsin cabin decorated to commemorate their lives and love as well as a grandson who died young. Outside the cabin, a large group of friends and family sat around a bonfire and small outdoor bar, celebrating, swapping stories, and, in quieter, more private moments, running a thumb along the edge of harder memories to see if they had gone dull. They rarely do.

I came to the gathering by chance and slow degrees, beginning back a decade or so when the man who owns the cabin and I were waiting in line at the local gas station during deer season. This was back when you had to haul your deer to town to register it, so the line was moving slowly, and we struck up a conversation. Time passed, and at some point the man started a lawn mowing service. One day our old mower disappeared in a blurt of blue smoke, and the man bailed us out with his equipment. This led to us shooting the breeze in the yard, that led to him lending me his torpedo heater to save my shed roof from the snow last winter, and that led to an invitation to the bonfire.

I don't want to overstep: The man with the cabin and I are on friendly and relaxed terms, but I am not his confidant. I can't really overshare, as I'm not privy to that level. Rather I carry the vision of those black-and-white photos beside the full-color snapshot taken a lifetime later, and how it causes me to view my own life in terms of decades rather than this afternoon's chore list. How we stood in that little room looking at the photos of the three departed even as the noise from the bonfire circle echoed across the yard, present evidence that the three lives represented remained cause for celebration off some county road among the dark Wisconsin pines.

You wonder in these moments what sort of bonfire you might precipitate, if any. Not the usual ephemeral monuments, the faded commemorations, the brass plaques for the young to pass by and briefly wonder who that was, and not even the full funeral home, but rather the stories passed around the flickering circle, the passing smile on the face of the person back in the shadows, the sparks and smoke rising as we toss another stick on the fire to keep it burning.

OL' WAYLON

For a long time I wanted to be Waylon Jennings. This was problematic, primarily because the job was already taken by Jessi Colter's husband. There was also the issue of not being able to chicken-pick a Telecaster, grow hair on the top of my head, or maintain the straight and narrow while inhaling Willie's secondhand.

Waylon Jennings is a bridge figure in my life. I was born too late to catch Buddy Holly on the radio but I came to know his music and his story in discovering after the fact that Waylon Jennings toured as Buddy's bass player and in fact lost the coin flip that put him on a drafty old bus rather than an ill-fated plane headed to ground in Iowa. First time I heard those Buddy Holly songs it was in a medley on the 8-track version of Waylon's "I've Always Been Crazy" album. I discovered the Beatles in parallel manner: When my high school math teacher showed up stricken to say John Lennon was dead, I wasn't sure who that was; then for the following week the radio played nothing but the Beatles and my back catalog education began.

You see, kids, he says, donning his curmudgeon cap, you couldn't just google this stuff in your palm.

That said, I spend a pretty good portion of my time these days trying not to be needlessly nostalgic. If my kids don't appreciate an LP crackle, or what joy we took from listening to the Top 40 in anticipation of who would land where because the stats weren't streamed and available in real time, I also know from driving those same children here and there with the radio or the phone playing pop songs I can't identify that the joy of discovering and identifying with music is not dead, it is just transforming. In his time the 18th-century playwright Voltaire packed theaters and was regarded as a genius; he also lived long enough to see the style that brought him fame fall into cheese.

Wherever I look—but mostly over my shoulder—there are signs warning me off the tendency to overindulge By-God-Back-In-My-Day syndrome. My past formed me, I am grateful for that past, and all change is not positive, but neither is getting a crick in your proverbial neck because you are forever looking backward.

This whole line of thought came about in a recording studio last week when a producer friend of mine suggested I try singing a little less like Waylon and more like myself. If I was Waylon I'd'a maybe snorted a line off the mixing board, kicked his amp in, tuned to Drop D and gone all extensively outlaw on his hinder. Instead I just grinned and prepared for Take Two.

The producer was right. Waylon lived that way so I didn't have to. I was never gonna be Waylon anyways. The very fact that I said "hinder" rather than—well, you know—proves it. And in his own way Ol' Waymore taught me that sometimes the most outlaw thing you can do is figure out how to ride into the sunset at a smooth canter rather than a mad gallop.

You can honor the past and even harmonize with it, said my producer friend, but you gotta sing your own song going forward.

LONER

I am an inveterate loner and pretty much have been since day one. Raised in a large family, I was born into two great privileges—love and stability—but the very size of the operation meant I was regularly left to my own devices. I spent long solo hours in the woods and ditches, driving tractor, and reading stacks and stacks of books up in my bedroom or out on the porch. I came to love solitude, whether I was truly alone, or simply alone in my head even in the midst of the day's happy tumult.

Yesterday we had a gathering at our farmhouse, an informal group of friends and relatives who arrived less by invitation than coincidence. I had been on the road for most of the previous two weeks and had come home in the wee hours and thus arose perhaps a tad after the roosters and in fact well after the guests had arrived. Some were out walking, some were picking tomatoes, others were chopping apples gathered from beneath our big tree.

Eventually—as with all the best get-togethers—everyone wound up in the kitchen. There were three or four conversations criss-crossing the countertop as the meal came together.

After the team prep, we moved to the dining room table and ate lasagna layered with tomatoes that only a few hours ago had lain whole in the sun. Meanwhile the scent of apple crisp drifted from the oven.

My wife is not a loner. Her heart is full when the house is full. I forget that sometimes, much to my discredit. In fact when we were dating, I often arrived to find her house filled with friends gathered for a meal. When I close my eyes and recall those moments what I see is her smile.

So much time has passed since then. So many chapters. So many days apart. And so many days together but quiet. And now this morning our kitchen filled with food and friends and noise and her smiling again.

At one point under the guise of fetching coffee beans I stepped out of the house and snuck up to my little workroom above the garage, where I sat in my old green chair for five minutes just to feel the silence. I was not unhappy, I was not hiding, I wasn't escaping anyone, I simply love the feel of solitude. Shortly thereafter, bag of coffee beans in hand, I returned to the house and its friendly noise.

As the coffee brewed, I looked around the kitchen. The conversation was once again running two or three separate threads. But the vibe was still united, and my wife was still smiling, and it occurred to me that my heart was feeling good in this mix, and we can too easily overdo our own mythology. I am indeed content when I am alone, be it by census or in mind. But it is possible to go stale in our own silence, and there is refreshment and joy to be had of sharing what's left of the garden and the windfalls and the words of others, and sometimes the self-declared loner is revivified by joining the crowd.

THREE BUCKS

This morning three whitetail bucks dallied just below the woodshed. Bucks gather up and start running together this time of year, and you know why. The last of the apples are off the tree, the morning air puts a little sniff in your nose, and the ungulate's eternal urge returns. Two of the bucks had small racks. They were out front, leading the way while the big guy hung back.

Deer are hardly rare around these parts. Nor does their presence necessarily connote remoteness. I've written previously about the friend who spent the entire day freezing in his deer blind on our back forty only to be obstructed on the drive home by a buck crossing the street in his suburb; the following night he phone-photo'd the deer posing beneath a speed limit sign. I've also watched a doe nurse her fawn mere feet from our front porch. This spring during a break in a thunderstorm I stepped out of my room over the garage and watched two tiny fawns cavorting on the wet driveway beneath a green tunnel of trees. At one point they got up on their hind legs and hoof-boxed. Fifty-four years and I'd never seen that before.

So deer in our yard are just slightly less common than chickens in our yard. But I also remember my youth, when we might go an entire fall and see but a handful of deer, let alone a trio of antlers, and so I called to my wife and we stood at the window to watch the bucks.

There was a lot of sniffing and posturing from the small pair. We couldn't see a doe, and apparently neither could they, but they were putting their noses to the air and curling their upper lips. I am told they curl the lip to trap and hold scent in the nostrils. Don't know if it's true but it's definitely the kind of thing you can drop into conversation down at the feed mill if you're looking to divert attention from the fact that your hands are soft and you type for a living.

The pair began to frisk, then started circling each other. Soon they were jousting, locking up their six-point racks and trying to twist each other to the ground. They separated, then came together again in a rattle of antlers.

Just when it looked like we'd see a legendary tussle, the two separated again and bopped off down the trail and into the brush. Perhaps they had scented a doe. Perhaps they were just skittery teens who couldn't maintain focus.

The big guy followed. He didn't trot or hop, he just kept a steady pace, following but maintaining his distance. My wife and I went back to our day, grateful for the simple diversion. Later it would occur to me that when those two finally did find a doe, they were in for a disappointment when Mister Big closed the gap and closed the deal.

SLEET WARNING

As the sleet hit my bald head I figured I better start a fire.

Around here a scatter of sleet balls doesn't scare us—last winter we carved our way to the chicken coop through snow canyons—but it does deliver a specific meteorological message regarding impending trends. I pulled a watch cap over my dome and trekked to the woodshed.

The woodshed is well-stocked as we approach winter. I'm tempted to brag on it except that this inventory is the product of a woodcutting bee organized by my wife and staffed by my relatives and neighbors. Also, because I resisted accepting their assistance the wood got rained on a couple times and isn't as dry as it should be. It'll burn, but it'll sizzle. Every bit of this paragraph except the opening line is a recurring pattern. If you squint back over time you can see life lessons and personal insights bouncing off my thick skull like so many sleet balls.

Earlier when I rode out the driveway to fetch my daughter from school the surrounding forest was a scrim of yellow cut with a vertical striping of dark tree trunks. The ambience was supplemented by a matching carpet smothering the asphalt.

There is a sweet spot of days when the ratio of leaves fallen to leaves remaining is in balance. It's a storybook look and if you switch the car radio off the very sound of the suspension is dampened.

We've pulled most of the squash and pumpkins from the weeds that swarmed the patch midsummer. Production was remarkably good despite overt neglect. In fact, other than getting foxtail seeds in my socks during the harvest, I can't say I have any regrets about spending my time writing rather than weeding. I think it's important to share gardening tips of this sort so as to take the pressure off some of you fellow under-achievers. Sometimes halfway up to snuff is enough. We also lost control of our tomatoes and they tipped their cages over and you know what? You'll neither suspect nor detect it when you blow the steam off your soup come January.

I started the fire, upping the kindling ratio so the damp wood would catch. Sure enough, there was some sizzle, but soon it was snapping right along. I halved some squash and began them to baking. Later that evening when we prepped the rest of supper, the old farmhouse was wood-fire warm and the squash had softened and filled the kitchen with a nutty scent. Outside it was getting dark, but the maple beyond the kitchen window—the one that doesn't just turn colors, it turns incandescent—was, in its own way, hanging in there, extending daylight as long as possible. There are moments when you understand the moment is all you have. You maybe checked in today on the toilet-bowl swirl of politics and public discourse and you look at that glowing tree and hope the trunk isn't hollow and the center is holding and it will put forth green leaves again next spring.

OLD GUY DISCOUNT

I take nothing for granted, but pending a terminal surprise, before the end of this year I will turn 55. In most cases I'm not a big birthday observor, but I've been looking forward to this one for a while and have big plans. *Business* plans, that is. In fact I am soliciting investors and am ready to take your money.

The entire project is predicated on the fact that when the sun rises on the anniversary of my birth I will become eligible for a wide range of discounts. I'm not sure if we still call them "senior" discounts, but I am less concerned with the terminology than the economic opportunity. The point is, simply by maintaining a pulse I will have earned big savings, or at least I will if I play this right.

Now then: While I'll be happy to claim a free small drink with my hamburger at your finer dining establishments where they hand the fine dining into your car through a window, my main discount focus will not be on myself. Is this because I am selfless? No, it is because I sense an opportunity for leverage.

It begins with my wife. She is ten years my junior and therefore unable to take advantage of old person discounts. I view it as my honor and duty to be that old person, standing beside her in the checkout line at various retail outlets and picking up the tab. She is a paragon of frugality and I hope this will make her love me more, especially since I am prone to leaving my ten percent discount socks on the floor. I am also trying to bank a little worth against any decline in other respects.

This is just family stuff, though. The real genius of my plan lies beyond heart and hearth. What I have in mind is an app-based discount shopper situation in which anyone ineligible for a senior discount and yet wishing to stretch their dollar will ping me with their location, I will show up to accompany them through the checkout, they get ten percent off, then I pocket a percentage of the ten percent. You can see the brilliance here. Making money off of other people's money.

I expect demand will be high, so naturally the app will have a cloud-based built-in reservation scheduler. This will maximize my availability and therefore my profitability. For an additional point or two I will make myself available for your entire shopping trip but you gotta push me in the little racecar cart.

This idea is too good to keep to myself, so I will be entering in to a franchise arrangement allowing other 55+ individuals to license the app. If all goes as planned, the venture capital will come pouring in, the enterprise will achieve "unicorn" status, and down at the feed mill they will speak of me in hushed tones as a "disruptor."

So far demand has been a little less than I might have hoped. Subscriptions for the beta-model are lagging to nonexistent. I still await my first angel investor. It wouldn't be the first time my genius has been overlooked. I considered offering a discount to anyone over 55, then did the math and realized there's a reason my genius is overlooked.

STORY TIME

It was called the Young Author's Showcase, so I didn't qualify. However, a young author of my acquaintance who wished to participate in the event weekend did not have her own driver's license, so I was allowed to sit in the audience as her chauffeur.

It was just the boost I needed.

Sometimes I think the aging process amounts to an accumulation of recurring themes. Some are timeworn and grumpy: Grousing about the cost of a stamp or the over-complication of coffee, absently pinching the new real estate above my beltline, or seething at anything that wastes my time—not because I deserve special treatment but because time-wise I am officially and statistically on the short side and getting shorter.

But then there are the unexpected and happier recurring themes. Among them: Regularly reacting with relief and a quiet smile when I rediscover how little I care about what brand are my pants, an ability to spot human fraudulence at a distance, and a tendency to utter the phrase, "kids these days!" more in hope than concern.

There is no doubt that a few of today's youth could do with more firewood stacking (hay bales an acceptable substitute, or really anything unexciting and heavy), more waiting (instant gratification has the pernicious effect of sharpening our hunger even as we consume, and is not limited to youth, I say, averting my eyes) and absolutely more boredom. That said, in the interest of keeping my nose in my own business, I rarely declare this outside of my own household.

But lately, more often than not, I find myself observing the youth of tomorrow in terms of hope. At the Young Author's Showcase, one writer after another took to the stage and proved they ain't all just stuck in their phones. That even during a life stage when they deserve time in their own little world, some kids these days are thinking of the bigger world, their place in it, the place of others in it, and the state of it. And beyond this planet, many of the young authors have created fascinating otherworlds in their heads and on their own terms, meaning kids these days still retain the ability to nurture other visions, not just those fed to them. And perhaps most important of all, every one of those who took the stage demonstrated that kids these days are willing to raise their own voice in their own way, a key reminder to this old chauffeur of the responsibilities implicit in my age.

I tend to get swept up in the moment. I suspect some of those young authors need to pick up their rooms. That they might have said something snarky or hurtful or less-than-poetic earlier that day. That some wisdom is available only through mileage. That "child-like" and "childish" have different meanings. I don't know what these kids will become over the long term. But from the stage of the Young Authors Showcase they put poetry in my ears, a challenge in my path, and hope in my heart. I remember not so much the words they wrote as how they delivered them: with brightness, with belief, and an eye on us oldsters.

HOTEL REVIEW

The van was low on oil so I grabbed a can at the big box store and topped it off in the motel parking lot. Then I checked the dipstick and realized I shoulda bought a chaser. Sometimes those idiot lights on the dash aren't crying wolf. And sometimes the idiot has been driving oblivious.

Dad raised me better than that. You want your equipment to last long enough to bring top dollar at the auction, he taught us, you grease it and park it beneath a roof. And if it's got an engine, check the oil before you start it.

Unfortunately, he raised an absent-minded goofball with pondering tendencies and furthermore they made those 2002 Toyota vans so bulletproof you can get away with some egregious inattention, especially if you're criss-crossing the dairy state sixteen ways to Sunday. At least now I know what that feathery clickety-click noise was when I'd hit the gas on the uphill. Sometimes our mechanic shakes his head so hard I feel like I should be covering his chiropractor bills.

Three nights ago I stayed in a real nice hotel. Someone else was picking up the tab, and I'll be sending them a thank

you note shortly. These last two nights, however, I'm footing
the bill, so I booked myself into a chain situation that has
treated me well for several decades of touring. More to the
point, I got a red-hot deal: two nights for less than one night
in that other place.

Sometimes there's a hard, cold reason you got a red-hot
deal. I stepped into the room and found it wreathed with the
overwhelming scent of bleach. And then, more disturbingly,
a second stratum of aroma just below the bleach that I could
not identify but had an organic redolence. I narrowed it down
to a couple of olfactory categories, neither of which put me in
a five-star state of mind. The cloud of creepy was further
enriched by the fact that the wall heater was left set at 85
degrees, recirculating the hot stench full-time.

I am Midwestern farm stock, so I hung in there. Didn't
want to complain. Know things are far worse all over the
place. All that humble church-pew shushing we were raised
on. But fifteen minutes in I felt like I was getting a headache,
and half an hour in, I had one. I went to the front desk and
requested a room change.

Room two presented with a wobbly mineral-encrusted
shower head, a rusty sink, petri stains on the chair and
carpet, several holes in the curtain and one in the bathroom
ceiling, but the sheets were clean and the air was clear so I set
up camp. As night fell there were squabbles and negotiations
in the parking lot. Someone tried to start a car over and over
and when it failed for good, screamed curses. There were
intermittent wall thumps.

I've lodged in sketchier situations. This was barely bottom
ten. I was gonna joke that the worst feature was I had to
watch the Packers lose on a low-res TV. Then this morning
the four people staying next door to me hauled two bags of
trash from their dented car to the dumpster and drove away

with the muffler dragging. Left behind in their parking spot was a pair of clean-rolled socks. Later when I picked up that second can of oil, it had the heft of luxury.

GETTING DIZZY

Yesterday as we drove past a playground I spotted a child spinning wildly on a centrifugal swing contraption and nearly lost my lunch.

The child was clearly joyful; arms tossed wide, head thrown back, a wide smile flashing at each rotation within a circle of other children helping to twirl her. They were all bundled in snowsuits; it was an enchanting scene, just the sort you'd hope children be allowed. And I had to look away. Of those childlike aspects of me that have survived adulthood, the joy of dizziness is not among them.

It was not always so. When I was small Grandma gave us a monkey swing for Christmas. It consisted of a red plastic disc with a hole in the center. The swing rode on a knotted rope threaded through the hole and looped over a limb of the white pine that towered above our sidewalk. Sometimes we swung on the monkey swing, but mostly we took turns spinning each other, hand-over-hand, as fast as we could manage. Then the swinger would climb off and try to run across the yard, veering and side-stumbling before finally pitching in to the grass. Hoots and giggles echoed off the barn.

In the house we'd pivot 'round and 'round and 'round, then try to climb up the living room floor as it rose before us, or try to put on the brakes as it slanted away. Other times we rolled ourselves across the lawn like logs before staggering and tumbling into the phlox.

Then at some point—as happens with so many adults— my physiology shifted and at the slightest revolution around my vertical axis I got green in the gills. My head would ache and my gorge would rise. Spinning 'round and 'round went from fun to foul.

So there went my figure-skating career. Ballet was out as well. These were never areas of emphasis, so I didn't feel too bad, but after watching a documentary on astronauts and fighter pilots in which they were spun on a giant centrifuge I realized I wasn't gonna get my wings or go to the moon, either. Once for a story about air shows I flew with an aerobatic team during an air show, and as we taxied to take off the pilot said, "If you throw up, you clean it up." I was proud that through barrel rolls, hammerhead stalls and loop-the-loops my stomach held its own, but any bravado evaporated when I climbed from the fuselage and staggered into the wing, so airsick I couldn't eat for 24 hours.

It doesn't take a stunt pilot to turn me green. I once took my younger daughter on a ride at the Northern Wisconsin State Fair consisting of cartoon bears that would rotate if you spun a disk in the middle, and after three spins I had to ask her to stop. When I dismounted all pale and wobbly, I recalled reading that figure skaters control vertigo by snapping their heads back in the reverse direction of their spin. I gave it a try. Now I was not only nauseated, I had a crick in my neck. My daughter charged off with her eye on some tornado-themed whirligig. Have fun, I said. Daddy's dizzy days are done.

KINDLING

The kindling was dwindling. In fact the old coal scuttle (are there *new* coal scuttles?) we use to carry kindling was down to sawdust when I started the fire this morning. Instead I used strips from a cardboard egg carton, an old wilderness trick I picked up from survivalist chicken farmers. It works, but your wood better be dry, and it better catch on the first try. There is no coaxing egg carton embers to life.

You want good kindling. It makes all the difference. You want thin strips of crackling dry wood to Lincoln-log atop the crumpled pages of the weekly shopper so that within seconds of the match-scratch, flames are curling and weaving betwixt the sticks, building the heat and momentum required to ignite the bigger chunks, some of which—if the resident wannabe lumberjack got behind again this year—may be a tad damp.

Good kindling is one of my favorite simple things and we are always running short. As with too many things in my life, I run on a just-in-time inventory system, meaning I am forever stumping down to the pole barn through snowdrifts to cut and chop another batch because we're out of egg cartons.

Today—for a few months anyway—I changed all that. I went down to the pole barn with the empty coal scuttle, made enough kindling to fill it, then didn't stop. I set up a production line composed of a roller stand and the radial arm saw, zipping board after board into brief lengths. Then I placed a sturdy, scarred old wooden table in such a position that when I split the wood atop it, the strips tipped into a large wooden catch-box on casters.

On my "just-in-time" runs, I always end up whacking some board with the chop saw, then kneeling on the concrete floor to do the splitting, an uncomfortable position worsened by being in an un-insulated steel shed in winter with the kids cold in the house, or me late to leave on some road trip but yet to dispatch my duty as the familial firestarter.

Today's session proceeded at a relaxed pace with the pole barn door wide open. There was residual snow in the grass but temps were balmy after a week of freeze. Wearing heavy leather gloves (typing is my life), I used my "boy's axe" (says so on the sticker I never took off) to do the splitting. I purchased it on purpose because a splitting maul is too heavy, and hatchets are like a sports cars...fun and zippy but tricky to drive. The boy's axe is heavy enough to force the split but light enough to make easy work, and the length is perfect for balance. I grip it halfway down the haft with the butt end tucked along the length of my forearm to my elbow. I don't so much swing it as simply dip it into the wood like a pump jack: *tunk, tunk, tunk* and the strips peel away.

The table was a key luxury. So much of the ease and efficiency of manual labor is predicated on surfaces. What a pleasure it was to stand up straight and just chop, chop, chop, knowing that with every descent of the blade I was prepping warm mornings weeks from now. That the kindling run would now be but a quick dash. That the overflowing cup is a messy blessing but the overflowing kindling box is simply warmth in store.

DANCE PARTY

At midnight the air was sizzling with lasers and thudding with music. The dance floor was elbow-to-elbow, and I was watching from the balcony, ready to head home. It had been one of those odd weekends I never saw coming when I left the farm for nursing school. Thirty-five years after cleaning my last calf pen, I found myself working at a two-day festival with and amongst musicians and dancers and sound engineers and caterers and roadies and fashion designers and composers and famous bass players, and if I did the full and deserved list we could fill the rest of this page and the entire dance floor.

My job was to write some things and speak some things and occasionally run some guitar slinger and his or her gear to an outlying venue. At one point I lugged a drum kit. I also gave a handful of performances in which I read excerpts from an essay about my truck while sitting in my truck. This is the sort of meta-mind-bending conceptual art that could really kick my career into high gear although the size of the cab dictates that the audience never exceeded two people, so I'm gonna have to pick up the pace bookings-wise. Also the very elements of the truck that render it charming also render it in no shape to travel more than fifteen minutes from home, so a lot of profit from the nationwide tour is gonna get eaten up by a tagalong tow truck. I would be remiss not to thank my 12 year-old daughter who assisted the art project by unloading all the firewood so I could park in front of the art center without tempting firewood thieves.

The truck sessions were a late addition. I hatched the concept on Saturday morning while sneaking a couple of hours in my deer stand before soundcheck. I wasn't sure how they'd go. After all, you're taking three people—a minimum of two-thirds who don't know each other—and jamming them shoulder-to-shoulder with their knees to the dashboard while one of us reads from a book. In the end it went great, and I would do it again if the passengers would.

But that had been hours ago, and now the week was catching up with me. When the laser band finished its final song, I went backstage, fetched my backpack, and returned through the venue toward the exit. The last of the dedicated attendees were clustered up around the stage. A new group of musicians were huddled over a table covered in laptops and other electronic gear at the center of a thunderous buzz saw of noise. I went out to my truck, started it up, drove home, and got my best night's sleep in a week. In the morning I walked out into the woods and just sat there. It was earthy and quiet. Somewhere the musicians were on airplanes and the late-night dancers were yet to rise. An hour later there was venison in the freezer. Been decades since I cleaned out a cow barn, but I'd grab a pitchfork tomorrow just to keep this weird little life rolling.

THE GOOD PEOPLE

I just spent a week working and performing with a fascinating batch of artists. Some from Paris and New York City, some from Eau Claire County, Wisconsin. Some famous, most not. It was an invigorating, challenging, uplifting, and disorienting (in the best sense) experience. Now they have scattered around the world (I scattered as far as Chippewa County to eat deep-fried turkey), leaving their work to echo where it will.

The experience heightened my sense of appreciation when—while searching for a photo from the festival, I came across another image emailed to me a couple weeks back. It was yours truly posed beside a man named George who—along with other members of his community—volunteers his time to study literacy with inmates at a county jail.

Several months earlier, George and his crew had invited me to share the privilege of meeting up and joining in for a session. I wedged the visit in during one of my unadorned minivan tours. This required a Rubik's cube-worth of coordination, but we found just enough time to divert and do it.

I've spoken in prisons and jails before, and my approach is to just show up and be who I am, a philosophy I also apply when speaking before high schoolers, as both audiences see through any false front at first glance.

My visit developed an unexpected complexity when we rounded a corner a mere 300 yards from the jail only to see a large banner promoting the candidacy of a circuit court judge with the exact same name as I. This turned out to be an icebreaker of sorts when one of the inmates led off the session by asking, if elected, would I reinstate their coffee privileges.

I rambled on about my background as a rural Wisconsinite and about writing as a form of self-employment not unlike logging only I never have to change out the head gasket on a monstrous feller-buncher over deer hunting in order to beat the blizzard as my brother recently had to do. I didn't try to be tough or cool. I can fake tough for just under 30 seconds and cool not at all. Instead I shoot for a straight-forward balance. Specifically, after casually dropping the term "feller-buncher" I referenced my amateur's affection for modern dance. Some cultural signifiers come clad in tire chains, others in ballet slippers.

A few hours with George and the fellows inside, then it was time to go. There was a moment of unintended humor at the end when without forethought, I said I had to hit the road, "And I know you guys have other things to do."

Everyone just stared at me, then busted out laughing.

Now, in the wake of a week of bright lights and microphones and flash and avant-garde and art oddities, it was nice to rediscover this photo of George and me, and remember all those like him, out there doing good where there is no spotlight. Doing good against all odds. Doing good even as so many are content to deceive or deride or derail. Sometimes it seems those losers are winning. And maybe they will. All the more reason to cherish the echoes left by George and his kind. And beyond cherishing, maybe add a little reverb of our own.

CHRISTMAS LISTS

It's that time of year when we are bombarded with Top Ten lists and asked to rank our own favorites: favorite holiday memory, favorite tree decoration, favorite Christmas present ever, and so on.

Problem is, I'm not good at remembering one-off things on the spot. I might tell you my favorite Christmas present ever was the handknit tin-can soda pop hats mom made for us, or the blow dryer grandma gave me when I was deep into my teenage appearance concerns, or the charcoal drawing set I got in grade school and loved to use on snowy days, but then a week later something jogs my memory and the Fred Bear recurve bow of 1978 slides to the top of the list...

So today when I tell you my favorite Christmas present ever was a trucker's logbook it's because that's the first one that came to mind as I looked out the window, saw snow falling and figured it was past time to cut the tree and bring it in so we can place some possible favorite presents of the future beneath it.

The logbook was a gift from my late Uncle Stan. As I recall he gave one to me and one to my brother John. I seem to remember a "to" and "from" in pen on the cover, his signature after the "from" reminding me of my grandpa's—his father's—penmanship, a nature/nurture study all its own. I remember I was deeply excited to get the logbook. All those blank pages. And CARBON paper. Pity those born into a copy and paste world too late to revel in such imperfect finger-smudging duplicative joys.

As a trucker, Uncle Stan would have seen the log book as a paperwork curse; as big brother and the DOT governing his throttle by both definitions. But he also understood the wonder and wander in our little hearts. He understood the way we viewed his giant roaring semi as a portal to worlds far beyond our Town of Sampson cow barn. He understood how these logbooks were a way to codify yearning, although he wouldn't in a million years have put it that way.

I remember Uncle Stan sitting down beside us, showing us how to graph out the flow of a day on the road, adding all the little marks and symbols and notations like he was diagramming the sentence of his trip. The sharp up-and-down of the line indicating when the truck was rolling, or when he was grabbing coffee in a diner, when he was out checking the tires or securing the load, and the names of faraway cities, some of which I'd only read about in the newspaper or, better yet, cowboy books.

Sometimes we used the gifted logbooks to chart our actual adventures. In particular I recall noting a submarine journey headquartered within an empty refrigerator box in the living room. I also remember sitting in my bedroom entering road trips that existed only in my mind, swearing I could smell diesel exhaust and western sage. In my imagination I could roll down the window, hear the engine roar, feel the sun on my arm. I was writing a novel using trucker terms.

That logbook was the best Christmas present ever. At least it was that day. Weirdly enough, just as I'm wrapping this up now I find myself wondering if the log book *was* a Christmas present. If I've misremembered and Uncle Stan just rolled up to the farm in his 18-wheeler on any given day, bearing these gifts simply because he understood their magic. I'm usually a stickler for fact-checking; in this case I've devised a workaround: I shall give myself the *memory* for Christmas. If Santa won't give me special dispensation, I trust the spirit of Uncle Stan will.

CHICKENS BACK ON BOARD

The chickens are laying eggs again, which seems a fine way to head into the new year. We're aware there are ways to keep them laying without pause, but prefer to follow the natural course of things as they keep our larder well-stocked the rest of the year and ask for little but kitchen scraps in return. In fact, I should make it a New Year's resolution to be half as productive as these birds.

No one is a bigger proponent of this natural hiatus than our younger daughter, whose after-school task it is to collect the eggs. This morning when I informed her that the laying boxes were once again populating the look on her face was a shade less than celebratory.

Our chicken flock census has dropped to its lowest since we got our first chicks. This is due to attrition and shifting priorities. I think we keep them because it's easier than getting rid of them, and also, there's nothing like an egg from a chicken that's been eating bugs and greenery. Even this time of year, when the green is gone and the bugs are all tucked away in the dirt or behind our siding, a home-laid egg still manifests a heartiness you won't find for cheap.

Folks sometimes want to argue about whether or not fresh farm eggs are any better for you than a watery store-bought, and my point is at that point you have missed the point. Leave nutrition to nutritionists, talking points to politicians, agendas to radio talk show hosts, and instead just go ahead and fry up a pair—maybe beneath a light dusting of Lawry's Seasoned Salt—and listen to your tummy. In issues of flavor, it's rarely helpful to out-think yourself. In less bucky tones, lemme just say above all I am *grateful* for these eggs, especially since they appear like magic daily, a remaining miracle you cannot download from the cloud.

I think right about now the younger daughter would request I tone down the miraculous rhapsodizing and focus a little more on how this morning I assigned her the duty of cleaning the nesting boxes, and how before the snow flew this fall she was allowed to clean the entire coop, and how it is she has to make that daily after-school trudge with the egg basket. But the true miracle of chickens is I want her to hit this world knowing how to run a pitchfork, how to do work that leaves you needing a shower, and even to understand that the shavings she lines the boxes with come from her grandfather the logger and lumber maker, and that the aroma of pine represents the intersection of honest work and nature.

I am getting melodramatic, but so be it. This world is uncertain, shifty, and sometimes deadly. The child slouching toward the coop has no idea how helplessly underqualified parents feel, and that sometimes the best we can hope to accomplish is to teach our children where breakfast comes from and how the world is full of unexpected excrement and yet we stay the course and do our chores and hope for the best, and pray come morning the sun rises to find the yolk lying yellow and lovely in the pan.

PACKERS GO BYE

The Packers arrived late against the Lions last weekend but managed to win and earn a playoff bye, so this Sunday they get to watch football as we do. I like the idea of multi-million dollar athletes slouched on a couch covered in nacho dust and picante stains yelling at kickers same as the rest of us furniture specialists. "My *gramma* coulda made that!" we screech, then doink it wide right off the trash can with our beer can. From half a yard out. And no 300-pounder lunging at us. Unless it's an uncle going for the final curd.

I loved football when I played it forty years ago. Now I simply enjoy watching it. I've come to kinda understand the game, whereas when I actually played it was without insight, using my muscles and wit but rarely my brain. I say wit because as an undersized offensive lineman I learned early that your average noseguard (as we called the central defensive lineman back in the day) came packing fifty extra pounds of beef but was often short on patience and repartee and could therefore be led down the path of iniquity with a few artful barbs, especially if the gibes arrived dipped in arcane multisyllabic esoterica.

I may have been a hayseed high schooler getting my head knocked in while long-snapping punts, but I read a lot of books, which meant I could perforate my opponent's non-football armor in low-key but specific ways often related to his self-perception. Having perhaps not read the Merriam-Webster for kicks, my opponents were prone to more standard comebacks, most of them a variation on one particular verb, the ultimate of which was indeed multisyllabic, but decidedly unoriginal and bound to catch the ear of the referee.

Having thus gotten the zebra's attention, I would quietly engage my opponent in conversation, often about his crest-fallen chromosomes or how the fast-twitch fibers in his legs came at the expense of slow-twitch fibers in his cerebrum or how his hypertrophied hypothalamus was likely crowding out his executive function. I always delivered these comments in a solicitous tone, as if I were speaking not in anger or pity but out of tender concern. This nearly always led to the opposing warrior spitting the same verb and pronoun over and over. When the time was right, I hit the punchline: "For such a large fellow you have a tiny vocabulary."

At this point he would punch me in the helmet. The ref—already keyed in—would toss him from the contest. In came the next guy, always a little smaller and a little slower.

Unfortunately, wits and running the 40 yard dash in 100 yard time will get you only so far on the gridiron, and by college I was done. I've watched far longer than I played, and have accumulated a decent working knowledge of the game. I wonder sometimes how our team would have fared had I possessed more strategy and technique as opposed to dumb adrenaline. If I had focused a little more on the playbook and a little less on the thesaurus. Go Packers.

WORLD EVENTS

World events have conspired to make me feel smaller than usual, and I wasn't feeling that big to begin with. I feel even smaller when I look at my children. Sometimes we speak of walking on eggshells, forgetting we live within one.

My job here is to turn in a story a week prior to it being published, leaving me at risk for looking more of a fool than usual. Last week I wrote a goofy piece about football and by the time it came out much bigger fuses had been lit. We have yet to learn how they might flare or sputter.

Here at ground level there is constant tension between maintaining awareness and maintaining our lane. This morning I lay in bed an extra fifteen minutes listening to a retired United States Navy admiral parsing various possibly pending scenarios related to current events. He spoke in measured cadence and steady tones. He said there would be trouble ahead but he also sounded like the sort of person you'd want in charge should trouble come. I note he is retired.

There came a commercial break after which he was to speak for another fifteen minutes, but the kid needed breakfast and so did the chickens, so I slugged out of bed and set about accomplishing the mundane.

I have never been grand. In neither my design nor my mien. I know a few big words and can sometimes arrange them prettily, but I am by definition a plugger, doing the best I can with a small toolbox containing mostly blunt objects. There are times when this feels useless and pointless. When I feel ashamed for not chucking it all and trying for something huge or loud or fiery. Then I look back in my toolbox and realize it is best to leave the billion-dollar battleships to the four-star folks.

That last line can be read as an excuse, or an exemption. I don't intend it as such, although it is the sort of statement worth pondering with a mirror at hand for the sake of honesty. One can self-deprecate oneself into obsolescence. I am speaking more in the moment. More as someone with a few basic skills and a family to feed, which puts me in the company of billions. More as someone putting a little lunch together for my daughter to eat between classes and play rehearsal, knowing that in ten minutes we will literally drop her off out there in the world, with even less than the usual eggshell in place.

This is one of those where I reach no grand conclusion. Where there is no ribbon of wrap-up. Where I am grateful for those whose toolboxes are stocked with remarkable implements of change or repair, and how I will put my shoulder to our little wheel here in hopes it will make it through the ruts and lend momentum to the larger carriage. Where we go about or days and go about our works, at once mindful and pragmatic, knowing history is rarely kind for long, so we must work our soft fingers into the hard cracks wherever we can, not to plug them but rather to pry them apart so the light flows through.

OLD PHONES

Boy, these kids and their phones...

Today I found myself crammed in a van with eleven other humans. We were en route to a major international airport. Before we squeezed in together we were waiting in the shuttle company lobby when a car pulled up and deposited a man at the entrance. He looked like a real lumberjack or perhaps a muleskinner. He stomped his boots and headed straight for the bathroom. Seconds later, he came slamming back out, gallumphing through our midst and into the parking lot, all the while roaring curses. Non-stop. All the biggies. Not a trace of public inhibition. Every syllable FCC-illegal except for two: "MY PHONE!"

It was a remarkable display. So remarkable in fact that one of the waiting passengers semi-jokingly asked the lobby attendant if we should seek cover, and the way we all swiveled our heads to gauge the attendant's response betrayed our true unease. To be clear: I once left my phone in the backseat of a taxi in Tucson and reacted in the very same way, although thanks to years of post-Calvinist Midwestern repression lessons, I was able to mute and disguise my terror. Turn it all inward, where it ate my liver.

Turns out—as he explained to the customer service rep loudly and profanely upon his empty-handed return—the man's hired ride had just driven off with his cellphone. Fast-forward and a few quick calls, and the car returned, and when the man packed into the shuttle with us he had his phone in hand.

And five miles down the road we *all*—save the driver, thank the rules—had our phones in hand. The couple beside me rode in silence, the wife doing Sudoku and answering texts from her sister (I know this because she would break the silence to update her mute husband). The fellow riding shotgun in his Navy veteran ball cap got loud alerts every minute or so which he responded to by shaking his head and grumbling and then poking at the phone face. Several other passengers were hooked to their earbuds, listening as they thumb-scrolled. I myself was checking email and texts, but of course my emails and messages were VERY IMPORTANT because I am VERY...yeah well I didn't really wanna talk either.

All but possibly two of the passengers were older than I, and I am early-stage Senior Discount eligible. I have also recently raised my first teenager in the age of the smart-phone. Thus it is my natural inclination, when I see anyone fiddling with their digital thumbsucker to do anything other than call mom or 911, to say, "Put that thing away!" Or—and this really doesn't work on the airport shuttle van, "HAND IT OVER...you can have it back in a week!"

So I held my tongue. I even shut my phone off for a few miles and meditated. As a koan I chose to focus on the laziness of assigning laziness to an age group. To wit, the easy maligning of millennials, many of which are my leading source of hope for our future. Sometimes they are doing good things with their phones and at this point my daughter is better at staying off hers while on deadline than I am.

How many of us are that man screaming for his phone like it was oxygen itself? I am not lecturing you. I am lecturing me. Because after a solid three minutes of phone-free meditation, I got a text and checked it immediately.

ARIZONA LOCKOUT

A brief bit of business took me to Tucson last week. I was grateful in many respects, mainly in that it is rare to see a saguaro socked in snowdrifts. I am culturally inclined to believe that Wisconsin winters build character, but how delicious it was to step outside on a fresh January morning to do sun salutations while wearing nothing but shorts, shower slides, and a light hoodie.

The hoodie was a nod to hair loss and reality, for despite the sun the desert was chilly. In fact, the air was cool enough on my bare legs and toes that I decided to pop back inside for socks.

Alas, I had locked myself out of the house.

Suddenly the air felt even cooler.

The house in question was a loaner. The owners were out of state. I had borrowed their spare key to get access. That key was now in full view through the window on a table not ten feet away from me—beside my phone, the car keys, and the keys to the garage.

I circled the house, wiggling every knob and testing every

sash. No luck. Although I was in a semi-developed area of the desert, the houses were low-lying and hidden, some with signage warning off sockless pale-legged losers in shower shoes.

I recalled passing a firehouse on my way to the property. With 30 years of firefighting and emergency responder experience as a conversational icebreaker, I figured maybe they'd let me use the phone—or a window punch. Failing that, the facility falls under Arizona's Safe Haven Law, which allows persons to transfer care of a newborn infant to firefighters and paramedics, no questions asked. Balding 55-year-olds don't qualify, but I figured they'd at least have to open the door.

And so off I went. It was slow going as plastic sandals load up with pea gravel every twelve feet, but eventually I arrived at the firehouse. I rang the doorbell. Nothing. Rang it again. Same. Earlier I heard a siren, so the crew was likely out on a call. I walked laps to stay warm.

Sure enough about twenty minutes in, a big fire truck pulled up. Shivering lightly, I greeted the crew at their own door. "Can we help you?" asked the crew leader, keeping his professional distance. From day one of rescue class we are drilled to ask ourselves, "Is the scene secure?" and to be fair my appearance was open to interpretation.

Ultimately they kindly invited me in. One lent me a cellphone and I made arrangements with a handyman to let me back in the house. For the next four days I never stepped outside without keys in my pocket and socks on my feet.

It never did get that warm in Arizona. But back in Wisconsin, fingers numb and nose hair frozen, scraping the ice off my windshield in a windblown, drift-clogged parking lot, it occurred to me that I am hitting that age where I prefer to build my character while lightly shivering in shorts. This notion is reinforced by my creeping belief that some people's character never improves no matter how cold it gets. And—to end on a happy note—my thanks to the day shift at Station X, who exhibited fine and welcoming character despite having shoveled not a single snowflake.

VOLTAIRE IS DEAD

This morning I rose at 5 a.m. and read the final chapter of Jean Orieux's *Voltaire*. This marks the end of a year-long tussle with the book, which is a 550-page pumpernickel loaf. I read it in fits and starts over the course of mornings and nights and sometimes lunch, marking it up as I proceeded. Knowledge retention has never been my forté (in high school and college I aced tests by cramming data that dispersed the moment I put down my pencil; consider me the intellectual equivalent of a dandelion) so I hope to give it a re-read one day and see if I still agree with myself.

It is helpful (albeit unnerving) to read all history against the present, and Voltaire provides lenses aplenty. The chapter I read this morning led off with the following quotation of the man: "There are two monsters that desolate the earth in peacetime: one is calumny, and the other intolerance; I shall fight them till my dying day."

"Calumny" is one of those words my dandelion brain retains just well enough that I think I know what it means but still look it up pretty much every time I cross it, and having done so again this morning I can tell you various dictionaries have it as the act of issuing false, malicious or defamatory statements about someone in order to damage their reputation. You get the feeling Voltaire would have been occupied with Twitter full-time.

In fact, that's a facile take (a dandelion brain specialty). As I—and others before me—have noted previously, Voltaire's predecessor Montaigne would have made a great blogger. Plato was the original content aggregator. These observations are cute but of limited use. At the moment I am focused on message over medium (a piquant perception in light of my typing this up as a newspaper column smack in our streaming age) and in Voltaire's time the Enlightenment was regularly swamped and swarmed by the dissemination of ideas through books and pamphlets, some corrupted by literary piracy, others curtailed by censorship, many driven by sensationalism, subversion, and insidious lies. It was the reader's responsibility to judge the messager as much as the message.

Through it all, Voltaire danced and defended his own truth. For the details, you'd be better off with Orieux than me. I enjoy reading about the man because he was susceptible to all human pettiness, spent a lot of time on financial investments as a form of insulation against politics and religion (and equal investments of strategic flattery), but also rose again and again to defend the highest ideals, often on behalf of those least likely to be allowed them.

Five hundred plus pages of Voltaire, and here is my takeaway: Few currents flow smoothly or directly, least of all human behavior, and for most of us row-boaters, navigation is the key. "What our eyes and mathematics prove to us must be considered true," wrote Voltaire, in the book's final quote. "As for all the rest, the only thing to say is 'I don't know.'"

Those last three words compose one of my top five favorite phrases; from Voltaire to Montaigne to Plato and the Socratic paradox. When I closed the book the sun was up and so were the birds. How lovely is a common peaceful day. If I am to look you straight in the eyes I must admit I googled "Socratic paradox" on my phone.

PARENT BRAKES

Among the unexpected complications of modern parenthood I failed to anticipate anti-lock brakes, which—when you finally lose it over the back-talk emanating from the back seat and power-stomp the pedal, intending to bring everything to a screeching and dramatic halt—give out with a wimpy *tack-eta-tacketa-tacketa*, easing the minivan through a rhythmic decrescendo, slowing it in increments until by the time you stop all the hot air has leaked from your drama balloon.

I should like to present myself as something other than that parent, but just because we would throw ourselves in front of a train for our children doesn't mean they don't sometimes drive us to consider that very act as a form of relief. The more deeply we love someone, the more likely they have access to our launch codes.

We all row through the ripples of our parents. In fact mine were loving and kind and constant and consistent, a blessing which is problematic because I fall short by comparison—although over the course of eighteen years I triggered both of them into uncharacteristic behavior just often enough that I know I'm not the first one to start a speech by stomping the brakes.

But anytime I catch myself going hair-trigger I automatically flash back to Mom and Dad and wonder how they'd have handled the moment. I am not them, I don't do everything they did the way they did, but they are the paradigm.

Back in the days when every penny shaved off the electric bill was dear, my father warned me if he found me asleep with a book over my face and the lights on one more time, he would remove my bedroom bulbs for two weeks. That night I dozed off reading as usual. The following evening I went to my room, hit the switch, and nothing happened. Fast forward thirty years and while unscrewing the light bulb my daughter has left lit after several warnings, I call Dad. "Guess what I'm doing!" I say, and we chuckle over the closing of a thirty-year circle.

We become parents and think we'll do it right. Won't fall into the standard caricatures. Won't ever holler, "Don't make me stop this car!" Then one day you glare lava-eyed into the rearview mirror and utter the very phrase. And get some sass. And now—because follow-through is everything—you gotta do it. But you're on the main thoroughfare approaching a stoplight, so first you gotta exit to the frontage road. This is a drain on your pizzazz. Meanwhile your blood pressure builds to a level measurable only by a trained volcanologist. Finally you are parked, and as you reach to yank open the door of the offending party, the key parenting tip I can provide is first make sure that door is unlocked. Vibrating in pain and confusion and possibly a Grade 5 shoulder subluxation, I spied my wife giggling in the passenger seat, and perhaps next week we will discuss parenting as a team sport.

NICHE JOKE

This week I made two jokes that won't play in every room. One (and to be clear the incident in question exceeded the statute of limitations many years and miles ago) referenced my two brothers moving a log cabin over three miles of public road at 3 a.m. via two hay wagons towed in parallel tandem by a tractor up front and braked by a pickup truck chained to the back. The brother on the tractor couldn't see the brother in the pickup, so when he wanted the brother in the truck to hit the brakes, he called him on his volunteer firefighter radio. When telling the story I always mention they took a test run around the hayfield first "because they're very safety-minded."

That line always gets a nice chuckle, and usually I leave it there, but last week I was speaking to a group familiar with big equipment, so after a beat, I added, "...and they both have CDLs."

It got an even bigger laugh.

There are several reasons for this, some having to do with timing and the flowing nature of laughter, but mainly it was because most of that audience knew "CDL" stands for Commercial Driver's License, which—if you are caught hogging the road in the conglomeration described above— the authorities will yank faster than a wig on a Jerry Springer rerun, and someone else gets to drive your log truck.

Or your grain truck; the room also slanted heavily toward agriculture, so during my presentation I reminded everyone that when you're driving a manure spreader, you should never switch the beaters on until you're headed *into* the wind. That one you can kinda figure out on your own even if the closest you've ever come to manure handling technology is a pink plastic kitty litter scoop, but in a room full of farm folk it gets an especially knowing guffaw.

That manure spreader line is over 20 years old. Its shelf life may be about up. In the time since I wrote it, the number of people who know what a manure spreader is, let alone what will happen if you switch the beaters on when you're running *with* the wind (put politely, you will incur aromatic precipitation) has dwindled significantly. I don't know what that says about my audience or the state of my speaking career, but here we are.

Lest I be accused of false humility, let me be absolutely clear that I am prepared to accept any fast lane break leading to an insufferable amount of loot. But in the meantime, I'm happy packing up the van, hustling my wares, and dropping asides understood only by what culture writers might refer to as "niche" audiences; librarians one week (an etymological aside worked with them), EMTs and nurses the next (you should hear the one about the emesis bag), a writers confer- ence after that ("STET!" is its own punchline), on and on, niche after niche, including, once, a convention of bovine artificial inseminators (those aren't going in the paper—see me after class).

Just checking, I see some Lutherans coming up on the calendar. Probably slip in the one about the time my brother attended a church basement funeral lunch and found himself sitting beside two elderly ladies raving about how good the food was when one of them said, "So who died?"

SLEDDING

We enjoyed one of those family get-togethers this weekend that had the driveway looking like a used car dealership. The house was a cacophony of games and chatter. Our two cats ran laps trying to escape the clutches of aggressively adoring children. The house was redolent of the gigantic ham heating in the oven, and the entire kitchen island was covered in dishes to pass. I made enough coffee to flood a lumberjack camp.

All this, and we were well shy of a full roster.

After lunch everyone bundled up and we hit the slopes, which is to say went sledding behind the woodshed. We've been on the farm a dozen years now, and usually manage one or two sledding parties a year. In the early days we stuck to the little slope over by the pole barn. Not much longer than a playground slide, it was perfect for many quick little trips. Now there are enough older kids they can help with the piloting and retrieval, so we run the bigger hill.

Conditions were perfect: a dusting of light stuff over a crust above a knee-deep base. The toboggan and plastic sleds skimmed swiftly, so well in fact that the adults had to ride along and bring things to a halt with their heels in order to keep the sleds from continuing on down-valley betwixt the spruce.

A couple of the older kids (including one about to finish his business degree but still awaiting certification in common sense) navigated through the powder all the way down the ravine and out of sight, leaving us to explain to the younger children begging us to follow, the difference between bravery and needless internal bleeding. In fact our reticence had less to do with the potential for injury than with the way our older thighs burned while tugging the empty sled up half the hill, never mind the whole hill.

After many joyous runs, everyone emerged rosy-cheeked and unharmed. We traipsed back to the house for games and cake but never got to the games, the kitchen conversation was that good. The kids amused themselves with singing, toys, and a movie, and resumed pursuing the cats. At one point my little niece emerged from a back bedroom with a cat hugged to her chest, its back feet dangling, its tail nearly to the carpet, and its face fixed in an expression of weary surrender.

"It jumped right into my arms," said my niece.

Yah, that's not entirely accurate, said the cat, with its eyes.

By dusk everyone was gone, and I went out to pick up the sleds. It's always quietly arresting to stand in the stillness after a day like that, all the energy of youth and action dissipated to wherever these things dissipate to, another day spent, the families traveling home in their various directions, the kids asleep in their car seats, sledding along through life, though as of yet they are blessedly free of such maudlin reflections, remembering only that it was a good day, there was cake, there was fun in the snow, and this is what it is to be good, good tired.

DOW WOW

I recently watched a documentary on Warren Buffett. This had very little effect on my net worth.

The documentary—which seemed non-sensationalized and thus perhaps accurate—put me in an unexpectedly reflective mood. This was due in part to interviews with Buffet's immediate family, none of whom spoke ill of him—in fact quite the opposite—but all of whom made it clear his priorities lay primarily with the market and what he and compound interest could make of it. I mention this only to say that while I may never catch him in the numbers-with-commas department, there have been long stretches when I easily matched his obsession with staying on task to the detriment of those around me. Buy and hold is pretty much the only way I'm wired to go. I don't get fancy with it, I just plow everything I've got into today's story, today's column, today's page, today's speaking gig, today's concert, today's whatever's-on-the-list, putting my faith in diversification and general accrual.

Lately that investment plan was taking a toll on the home front. Nothing dramatic to report, just one of those times when you recognize it's time to review the portfolio and do some fiduciary due diligence. See how the profit-to-expense ratio tallies up. Make sure you're not overweight on buckle-down and underweight on loosen-up.

It is a blessing to discover what you love to do and then be allowed to do it. I'd say that pretty much happened with me by the time I was twenty-five. That doesn't mean I'm happy every day. That doesn't mean every day is productive, or even fulfilling. It just means when I roll out of bed I know what I want to do and most days am allowed time and opportunity to do it. Warren Buffet, the same. He gets in his car and drives from his simple home in Omaha to his office in Omaha, stopping in between to get breakfast through his car window at McDonalds. What I take from this is that Warren doesn't want the fancy stuff, he just wants to do the stuff. It is exactly how I feel every morning, give or take a few billion dollars. And I happen to know it is the same for my brother the logger.

I regularly use my brother the logger as a point of reference. Somewhere between him and Warren Buffet I work my little groove. It's all well and good to be aspirational, but it's also good to feel satisfaction right here where you're at. To take a little time off chasing deadlines and maybe instead sit down with your spouse. At a place where they have the TV channels you don't have at home. And where you're secretly glad she was asleep when you watched the parts where Warren's family matter-of-factly acknowledged he'd rather work than play.

After the recent stock market fluctuations, I don't know if Mr. Buffet remains in the running for the world's richest man, but he's got a solid lead on me. It's fine. Today the Dow Jones dropped a thousand points. I went ahead and wrote this column anyway.

BLITHE

These are not blithe times, nor is it a time to be blithe, but as I so often say in my opening salvo, I'm writing this seven or eight days in the past, so sometimes you just gotta drop the plow and go. If nothing else I am forced to consider each week how the words I type will sound depending on contemporary circumstances.

But, yep. Then you just gotta get the typing done and get ready for the next thing. As of now I am in the passenger seat of my old van, my friend Ben doing the driving as we set out on a little mini-tour of the state, the books and CDs and a couple guitars packed in the back, and the rest of the material riding in my head. Right before we left, quite literally as we were getting into the van, I slipped on the ice and came within two degrees of bouncing said head off the blacktop like a melon in a David Letterman sketch.

Does anyone remember? When David Letterman used to drop watermelons and other random objects from the top of a building just so we could watch them smash? Oh, it was pointless and delightful. Especially the shot from above, the melons waning in slow motion, then starbursting across the asphalt like juicy one-dimensional fireworks.

Sometimes, just to mix it up, he hired a steamroller and ran things over. Boomboxes, fruit, footballs. This too satisfied a lot of suppressed urges.

Silliness, pure and simple. But you notice how for two paragraphs there we managed to forget about the stock market and the assorted underqualified bloviators in charge of our future? I got no answer for you there, but the mind-vacation was fun while it lasted.

Mind, melon, silliness; what sent me down this track was the idea that had I tipped those additional two degrees on the ice beside the van and cantalouped my brain-pan in the Letterman style, the show would have quite literally been over, and that would have been goofy on the face of it, because although I just took a shot at the knuckleheads reigning over us, I'm not exactly an organizational genius myself, and yet somehow the overcharged and underpowered ping pong balls of my mind have lined up long enough over the years to produce a product that generates a living for my family and regular part-time employment for a number of other freelance talents.

How silly then, that the whole enterprise depends on me quite literally keeping my head together. When you're an actual business bigshot—say at some red-hot tech company —you are required to take out "key man" insurance for that very reason, the terms of which strictly prohibit certain activities like parachuting or snowboarding or partying on yachts owned by the Russian mafia. Despite my critical role in our little operation, no one has ever tried to hook me up with key man insurance, plus if you attached a rider prohibiting walking on ice on any given winter Thursday in Wisconsin, well, I just wouldn't make it to the gig.

As it turns out, none of this is blithe, but is all very silly, so I'll bring it to an end. Plus, we're about to pull into the venue. I may be the key man, but I still gotta help Ben unload the van. Off I go, thoughts intact, and one eye out for the slippery spots.

THE OLD STORIES

For the first time in seven years, there are no teenagers in the house. The elder child just turned twenty, and the youngest is pre-teen for a few more weeks. I find myself wanting to stand athwart time and holler whoa.

All these years as a party of four, and last night it was just the three of us driving home from the regularly unscheduled Sunday night popcorn dinner get-together up north at the family farm. It was one of those visits that highlight the passage of time—my parents nearing their 80s, my elder child away at college, the bulk of the tales shared around the room having taken place four or five decades in the past—and yet as I sat at the kitchen table of the home I was raised in I still felt the space like it was me—rather than my daughter—who was twelve.

One of my ongoing latent hobbies is time travel. I haven't figured out how to actually physically manifest anywhere than right here in the lumpy moment, but I enjoy circumstances or stimuli that transport the well-worn me back to the fresh-faced me, if only in my mind. I recently caught a whiff of sage and suddenly I was 18, tanned and trim, and halfway through a day's work on the Wyoming prairie that would leave me solidly worn out and solidly satisfied in a way I often still seek. That memory led to the squeak of the linoleum in the cookhouse where all the hands gathered for breakfast, which reminded me of the tureens of scrambled eggs and the first time I followed the example of my boss and slathered them with picante sauce—pretty big stuff for a Wisconsin boy who up 'til then had run pretty much mild cheddar. From there my mind drifted into how my feet thudded as I left the cookhouse and crossed the wooden bridge toward the horse barn where a telephone mounted to a post was made available to the hands who might have wanted to call their parents or a sweetheart on a Sunday, the long distance charges neatly deducted from your monthly paycheck.

You take a mind-trip like that, it's a little jarring to hear a ping on the phone and remember you forgot to renew the license plate on the family minivan. In fact, time travel is a tricky business. Too much dwelling in the past, too many times the same story retold, and you're just mooning, mourning, and moping around about the state of things these days. At one point during all the storytelling I looked over at the child on the cusp of her teens, just sitting there. She has reached the age where she is regularly impatient with the oldsters. I wondered how bored she must be with our rehashed memories.

Then on the road home, without prompting, a voice arose from the darkness in the back of the van. "I love to listen while you all talk about growing up. It helps me understand what it was like. And it's fun to know how you were when you were young."

Tell your stories. Youth is bound to leave us behind, but so it is they carry us along. There is something in my eye.

THE HEALING DAY

Lately I've been leaning pretty heavily on "The Healing Day," a song by Bill Fay. It's a gentle number. Somewhere between lullaby and hymn. Fay was 69 years old when the song was released, and it's a good thing, because it's a piece whose proper delivery requires some prior living. I've known some fine studio hands, and Auto-Tune's a wonder, but you can't chef up empathy.

Fay sings as if he's smoothing a child's brow. *It'll be okay*, he sings, barely above his breath, his voice acknowledging the darkness all around even as he breathes his belief in the light. I hear it and think of the times I have sat on the edge of my own child's mattress, doing my best to soothe the small creature when thin threads of dread hung above the bed. How many times do we hold our children close under the guise of comforting them when in fact we are clinging to them as if they were the last buoy in a cold sea?

"The Healing Day" lands on my ears as an unanswerable conundrum. The flat-footed, clear-eyed, windburned part of me knows no song so fragile, sung by a voice so frail, can withstand—let alone overcome—these hardhearted days. Or the vicious fools among us. You would do just as well to block a bulldozer by propping a blown glass ornament against the blade. And yet I accept the comfort of the song, because the comfort is real. It is ephemeral, but then in the big picture, so are bulldozers.

Every battleground, sings Fay, *is a place for sheep to graze.* Nine words acknowledging the damage we humans do ourselves, conveying the implication that some of us will not survive, or escape unscathed, but allowing that one day the blood and dirt will grow up in pasture. It is the perfect image; no animal grazes unless it feels safe. Forty years my dad raised sheep; Fay sings and I see them, flocked and cropping grass in the mist.

Last night in bed I read a pair of Wendell Berry profiles. Berry is 85 and still working his dozen acres. Less than before, but then he's got plenty of labor banked. I found myself growing impatient with some of his insistences. Not because I think he's wrong, but because I don't see how enough of us can be Wendell Berry. Because I don't see how a couple tending twelve Kentucky acres is a credible bulwark against —let's go ahead and run the tracks off this metaphor—the bulldozer of consumer demand and simple venal greed. The disciples are outnumbered.

But there was something in Berry's words that plucked a harmonic in my subconscious. It took me a bit, but after I snapped the bedside light off, it came to me: I was sensing the interplay between Berry's words and Bill Fay's music. Both men understand the battle is pitched against gentler folk, but peaceful persistence is its own reward. It isn't a matter of winning, it is a matter of dignity. *Be at peace with yourself,* sings Bill Fay in another song, and at the edge of sleep I recite those words against the universe, hoping my children will hear them.

ABOUT THE AUTHOR

Michael Perry was raised on a small dairy farm, worked as a ranch hand in Wyoming, got a nursing degree, then wound up writing and performing for a living. Just happy to be here.

At the time of this printing, he lives with his wife and two daughters in rural Wisconsin.

If time and technology allow, visit SneezingCow.com for dispatches, photographs, and video.

And thank you.

Made in the USA
Coppell, TX
01 December 2020

42682234R00143

汉语风　中文分级 Chi...
系列读物 Grade...

cuò　　cuò　　cuò

错，错，错！（第二版）

Wrong, Wrong, Wrong!

主　编　刘月华（Yuehua Liu）　储诚志（Chengzhi Chu）

原　创　赵绍玲（Shaoling Zhao）

北京大学出版社
PEKING UNIVERSITY PRESS

图书在版编目（CIP）数据

错，错，错！/刘月华，储诚志主编. —2版. —北京：北京大学出版社，2017.5

（汉语风中文分级系列读物）

ISBN 978-7-301-28251-9

Ⅰ.①错… Ⅱ.①刘…②储… Ⅲ.①汉语—对外汉语教学—语言读物 Ⅳ.①H195.5

中国版本图书馆CIP数据核字（2017）第085219号

书　　　名	错,错,错!(第二版)	
著作责任者	刘月华　储诚志　主编	
	赵绍玲　原　创	
责 任 编 辑	李　凌	
标 准 书 号	ISBN 978-7-301-28251-9	
出 版 发 行	北京大学出版社	
地　　　址	北京市海淀区成府路205号　100871	
网　　　址	http://www.pup.cn　新浪微博:@北京大学出版社	
电 子 信 箱	zpup@pup.cn	
电　　　话	邮购部 62752015　发行部 62750672　编辑部 62753027	
印 刷 者	北京大学印刷厂	
经 销 者	新华书店	
	850毫米×1168毫米　32开本　2.625印张　41千字	
	2007年11月第1版	
	2017年5月第2版　2019年9月第2次印刷	
定　　　价	20.00元	

刘月华

毕业于北京大学中文系。原为北京语言学院教授,1989年赴美,先后在卫斯理学院、麻省理工学院、哈佛大学教授中文。主要从事现代汉语语法,特别是对外汉语教学语法研究。近年编写了多部对外汉语教材。主要著作有《实用现代汉语语法》(合作)、《趋向补语通释》《汉语语法论集》等,对外汉语教材有《中文听说读写》(主编)、《走进中国百姓生活——中高级汉语视听说教程》(合作)等。

储诚志

夏威夷大学博士,美国中文教师学会前任会长,加州大学戴维斯分校中文部主任,语言学系博士生导师。兼任多所大学的客座教授或特聘教授,多家学术期刊编委。曾在北京语言大学和斯坦福大学任教多年。

赵绍玲

笔名向娅,中国记者协会会员,中国作家协会会员。主要作品有报告文学集《二十四人的性爱世界》《国际航线上的中国空姐》《国际航线上的奇闻秘事》等,电视艺术片《凝固的情感》《希望之光》等。多部作品被改编成广播剧、电影、电视连续剧,获各类奖项多次。

Yuehua Liu

A graduate of the Chinese Department of Peking University, Yuehua Liu was Professor in Chinese at the Beijing Language and Culture University. In 1989, she continued her professional career in the United States and had taught Chinese at Wellesley College, MIT, and Harvard University for many years. Her research concentrated on modern Chinese grammar, especially grammar for teaching Chinese as a foreign language. Her major publications include *Practical Modern Chinese Grammar* (co-author), *Comprehensive Studies of Chinese Directional Complements*, and *Writings on Chinese Grammar* as well as the Chinese textbook series *Integrated Chinese* (chief editor) and the audio-video textbook set *Learning Advanced Colloquial Chinese from TV* (co-author).

Chengzhi Chu

Chu is associate professor and coordinator of the Chinese Language Program at the University of California, Davis, where he also serves on the Graduate Faculty of Linguistics. He is the former president of the Chinese Language Teachers Association, USA, and guest professor or honorable professor of several other universities. Chu received his Ph.D. from the University of Hawaii. He had taught at the Beijing Language and Culture University and Stanford University for many years before joining UC Davis.

Shaoling Zhao

With Xiangya as her pen name, Shaoling Zhao is an award-winning Chinese writer. She is a member of the All-China Writers Association and the All-China Journalists Association. She authored many influential reportages and television play and film scripts, including *Hostesses on International Airlines*, *Concretionary Affection*, and *The Silver Lining*.

前　言

　　学一种语言，只凭一套教科书，只靠课堂的时间，是远远不够的。因为记忆会不断地经受时间的冲刷，学过的会不断地遗忘。学外语的人，不是经常会因为记不住生词而苦恼吗？一个词学过了，很快就忘了，下次遇到了，只好查词典，这时你才知道已经学过。可是不久，你又遇到这个词，好像又是初次见面，你只好再查词典。查过之后，你会怨自己：脑子怎么这么差，这个词怎么老也记不住！其实，并不是你的脑子差，而是学过的东西时间久了，在你的脑子中变成了沉睡的记忆，要想不忘，就需要经常唤醒它，激活它。"汉语风"分级读物，就是为此而编写的。

　　为了"激活记忆"，学外语的人都有自己的一套办法。比如有的人做生词卡，有的人做生词本，经常翻看复习。还有肯下苦功夫的人，干脆背词典，从 A 部第一个词背到 Z 部最后一个词。这种做法也许精神可嘉，但是不仅过程痛苦，效果也不一定理想。"汉语风"分级读物，是专业作家专门为"汉语风"写作的，每一本读物不仅涵盖相应等级的全部词汇、语法现象，而且故事有趣，情节吸引人。它使你在享受阅读愉悦的同时，轻松地达到了温故知新的目的。如果你在学习汉语的过程中，经常以"汉语风"为伴，相信你不仅不会为忘记学过的词汇、语法而烦恼，还会逐渐培养出汉语语感，使汉语在你的头脑中牢牢生根。

　　"汉语风"的部分读物出版前曾在华盛顿大学（西雅图）、范德堡大学和加州大学戴维斯分校的六十多位学生中试用。感谢这三所大学的毕念平老师、刘宪民老师和魏莘老师的热心组织和学生们的积极参与。夏威夷大学的姚道中教授、加州大学戴维斯分校的李宇以及博士生 Ann Kelleher 和 Nicole Richardson 对部分读物的初稿提供了一些很好的编辑意见，在此一并表示感谢。

Foreword

When it comes to learning a foreign language, relying on a set of textbooks or spending time in the classroom is not nearly enough. Memory is eroded by time; you keep forgetting what you have learned. Haven't we all been frustrated by our inability to remember new vocabulary? You learn a word and quickly forget it, so next time when you come across it you have to look it up in a dictionary. Only then do you realize that you used to know it, and you start to blame yourself, "why am I so forgetful?" when in fact, it's not your shaky memory that's at fault, but the fact that unless you review constantly, what you've learned quickly becomes dormant. The *Chinese Breeze* graded series is designed specially to help you remember what you've learned.

Everyone learning a second language has his or her way of jogging his or her memory. For example, some people make index cards or vocabulary notebooks so as to thumb through them frequently. Some simply try to go through dictionaries and try to memorize all the vocabulary items from A to Z. This spirit is laudable, but it is a painful process, and the results are far from sure. *Chinese Breeze* is a series of graded readers purposely written by professional authors. Each reader not only incorporates all the vocabulary and grammar specific to the grade but also contains an interesting and absorbing plot. They enable you to refresh and reinforce your knowledge and at the same time have a pleasurable time with the story. If you make *Chinese Breeze* a constant companion in your studies of Chinese, you won't have to worry about forgetting your vocabulary and grammar. You will also develop your feel for the language and root it firmly in your mind.

Thanks are due to Nyan-ping Bi, Xianmin Liu, and Ping Wei for arranging more than sixty students to field-test several of the readers in the *Chinese Breeze* series. Professor Tao-chung Yao at the University of Hawaii. Ms. Yu Li and Ph.D. students Ann Kelleher and Nicole Richardson of UC Davis provided very good editorial suggestions. We thank our colleagues, students, and friends for their support and assistance.

主要人物和主要地点
Main Characters and Main Places

林双双 Lín Shuāngshuāng
Elder sister of Lin Duidui

林对对 Lín Duìduì
Younger sister of Lin Shuangshuang

李亮 Lǐ Liàng
A police officer

王明 Wáng Míng
Another police officer

陈飞 Chén Fēi
A man with whom both Lin Shuangshuang and Lin Duidui
fell in love

王美美 Wáng Měiměi
A good friend of Lin Duidui and Lin Shuangshuang

北京 Běijīng: A city you know!

上海 Shànghǎi: Another city you know!

锦江饭店 Jǐnjiāng Fàndiàn: Jinjiang Hotel in Shanghai

文中所有专有名词下面有下画线，比如：林双双、北京
(All the proper nouns in the text are underlined, such as in 林双双、北京)

目　录
Contents

1. 有一个小姐死[1]了

"有一个小姐……死[1]了！她在地上[2]，在房间[3]的地上[2]……她像在睡觉。她很漂亮，但是她……她已经死[1]了！"

打电话的男人说话有点儿快。听电话的是警官[4]<u>李亮</u>。

5

1. 死 sǐ: die
2. 地上 dìshang: on the floor
3. 房间 fángjiān: room
4. 警官 jǐngguān: police officer

这是在中国的北京，这一天是6月9号，星期五，时间是上午11点15分。三分钟[5]前，<u>李亮警官[4]</u>的大学同学给他打来一个电话说，给他介绍了一个女朋友，<u>李亮</u>打算明天晚上和她见面。

"在那儿等着，不要让人进去！"<u>李亮警官[4]</u>说完，马上跟<u>王明警官[4]</u>一起走出房间[3]，上了汽车，他们要很快到死[1]人的地方去。

5

10

Want to check your understanding of this part?
Go to the questions on page 54.

5. 分钟 fēnzhōng: minute

2. 第一个证人[6]的话

那个地方很不错，像个大公园，那里的房子很大，也很好看。那个小姐是在一个最漂亮的小红楼里死[1]的。中午的天气很热，打电话的男人拿着信，在小红楼前边[7]走来走去[8]，看见[9] 李亮警官[4]和王明警官[4]的汽车，他马上跑过来。

"我是打电话的人。"他对警官[4]们说，"今天上午10点，我来这里给林对对送信"。他给李亮警官[4]看他要送的信。信上写的字很漂亮，寄信的人叫陈飞，应该是一个男人的名字。

"我来的时候，房子的门[10]是开着的，我就说：'请问，林对对在家吗?'没有人说话，也没有人出来，但是我听到房子里有电视的音乐，所以

5

10

15

6. 证人 zhèngrén: witness
7. 前边 qiánbian: in front
8. 走来走去 zǒulái-zǒuqù: pace, walk up and down
9. 看见 kàn jiàn: catch sight of, see
10. 门 mén: door, gate

我又说：'请问<u>林对对</u>在家吗？'还是
没有人说话，没有人出来……我想知
道为什么房子的门¹⁰开着，电视也开
着，但是没有人出来，就从开着的门¹⁰
5　往里边¹¹看了一下，就看见⁹那个小姐
躺¹²在房间³的地上²……"

"你认识她吗？"<u>李亮</u>警官⁴问送信
的男人。

"不，不认识。我常常给她们送
10　信、送礼物，但是我不认识她们。"

"她们？"<u>李亮</u>问。

"是的，她们。她们是孪生¹³姐

---

11. 里边 lǐbian: inside
12. 躺 tǎng: lie down
13. 孪生 luánshēng: twinborn

妹[14]。她们的名字一个叫<u>林双双</u>，一个叫<u>林对对</u>。我看见[9]过她们，但是有意思的是，我不知道她们谁是<u>林双双</u>，谁是<u>林对对</u>。她们两个人长得非常像。她们穿的衣服常常是一样的，头发[15]也一样，她们看起来[16]就像一个人一样。"

5

"她们的信很多吗?"<u>李亮</u>问。"很多。这个叫<u>陈飞</u>的先生常常给她们写信送礼物。两个月前，他常常给<u>林双双</u>写信送礼物，现在常常给<u>林对对</u>写信送礼物。"

10

14. 姐妹 jiěmèi: sisters
15. 头发 tóufa: hair (on the head)
16. 看起来 kàn qilai: seem, look like

李亮和王明走进那个小红楼。他们看见[9]电视开着，有人在电视里高兴地唱着。房子里的东西都很新，很漂亮，也很贵。李亮想，这姐妹[14]两个人一定很有钱。

死[1]了的那个小姐躺[12]在一个房间[3]的地上[2]，像在睡觉，她的身体前边[7]有一个杯子[17]，杯子[17]里有一些[18]水。她非常漂亮，可是脸[19]很红，李亮和王明看了，马上就知道，这是因为喝了一种不好的药，那种药叫氰化物[20]。喝了氰化物[20]的人，死[1]后脸[19]都很红。

李亮还看见[9]那个小姐的衣服上有个东西。他拿起来看了看，是信，信很短，信上写着几个字：我很累，我走了。下面[21]写着名字：林双双；还写着时间：6月8号。

李亮警官[4]看完了房间[3]，拿出一个本子[22]，在本子[22]上写下听到和看到的这些[18]事情[23]：

17. 杯子 bēizi: cup, glass
18. 些 xiē: some, few, several
19. 脸 liǎn: face
20. 氰化物 qínghuàwù: cyanide, prussiate
21. 下面 xiàmian: below, under, underneath
22. 本子 běnzi: notebook
23. 事情 shìqing: thing, matter

　　今天是6月9号，星期五，上午11点15分，一个送信的男人看见⁹一个小姐在家里死¹了。这个家里有两个孪生¹³姐妹¹⁴，姐姐叫林双双，妹妹²⁴叫林对对，她们长得非常像，看起来¹⁶像一个人一样，人们²⁵常常不知道她们谁是姐姐双双，谁是妹妹²⁴对对。

　　昨天，不知道为什么，姐姐双双死¹了，她死¹的时候躺¹²在家里的地上²；人们²⁵找妹妹²⁴对对，但是不知道她在哪里。有个叫陈飞的男人，两个月前常常给姐姐双双写信送礼物，

5

10

24. 妹妹 mèimei: younger sister
25. 人们 rénmen: people, the public

现在喜欢给妹妹[24]对对写信送礼物……姐姐林双双自杀[26]了，是不是因为那个叫陈飞的男人不喜欢自己[27]了？可是因为她们太像了，那个送信的人不知道死[1]的是姐姐双双，还是妹妹[24]对对。

5

李亮还在本子[22]上这样写：

10

那个小姐的衣服上有个东西，那是信。信上告诉人们[25]她是自杀[26]的，信上写着的名字是林双双，但是事情[23]不一定真是这样。

15

这个死[1]了的小姐真的是林双双吗？她真的是自杀[26]吗？李亮和王明心[28]里都在想着这样两个很难的问题。

Want to check your understanding of this part?
Go to the questions on page 54–55.

26. 自杀 zìshā: commit suicide
27. 自己 zìjǐ: oneself
28. 心 xīn: heart, mind

8

"啊……这是怎么了?!"一个五十多岁的女人大叫着跑来，中午的天气很热，她的脸[19]很红。

"啊，这个女人的脸[19]真红，也像喝了氰化物[20]一样!"李亮想，"同学给我介绍的那个小姐一定不要像她这样，我不喜欢这样红的脸[19]!"李亮这个时候想到了他的新女朋友。

那个五十多岁的女人是这个家里的保姆[29]。看见[9]死[1]在地上[2]的小姐，老保姆[29]马上大叫起来："对对，对对，你怎么了?!"

"等一等，你叫她对对? 你怎么知道她是对对，不是双双?"李亮说。

"因为这是对对的房间[3]，警官[4]先生。"

"你知道这是谁的杯子[17]吗?"李亮拿着那个有一些[18]水的杯子[17]给老保

5

10

15

---

29. 保姆 bǎomǔ: nanny, housekeeper

姆[29]看。老保姆[29]看了看那个杯子[17]，马上说："我认识这个水杯，这是对对的。"

"为什么？"李亮问。

"你知道，双双和对对的东西都是一样的，她们喜欢买同样[30]的东西，她们的爸爸妈妈也喜欢给她们买同样[30]的东西。这两个水杯就是她们的妈妈给她们买的，所以，姐妹[14]两个人都有一个这样的水杯。这两个水杯看起来[16]是一样的，但是，双双的水杯这里有一点儿红，这个水杯这里没有红的东西，所以我知道这是对对的

30. 同样 tóngyàng: same

水杯。"

　　"她知道的事很多。"李亮高兴地对王明说，"我们应该请她告诉我们一些¹⁸新的、我们不知道的事。"

　　老保姆²⁹在这个家工作八年了，这个家里的很多事她都知道。

　　"这两个孪生¹³姐妹¹⁴都很漂亮。"保姆²⁹说。"她们的爸爸妈妈很有钱，他们也给这两个孩子很多钱。看，那就是他们的照片。"李亮和王明看见⁹照片上有一个五十多岁的男人，还有一个四十多岁的女人，他们坐在漂亮的小飞机上，很舒服的样子³¹。那个女人非常好看，李亮想，这个死¹了的小姐很像这个女人。

　　"两年前，他们去外国旅行。他们想看一些¹⁸外国的新药，那是他们的工作。但是飞机出事³²了，他们没有回来……所以他们的这个红楼和钱就都是双双和对对的了。"

　　"你想一想，昨天在这里看见⁹什么了？"李亮问老保姆²⁹。

　　"昨天上午我去买菜，11点我拿

31. 样子 yàngzi: appearance, shape
32. 出事 chū shì: have an accident

着菜来给双双和对对做午饭。我刚走
进房子，不知道是双双还是对对跑了
出来，对我说，'你今天早点儿走吧，
今天不用做午饭了，我们有点儿事，
要马上回大学去。'"

5

"等一等，你说，你不知道跑出来
的是双双还是对对?"

"是的，我不知道。她们两个人太
像了！她们长得一样高，一样漂亮，
她们都喜欢音乐，喜欢说英文，喜欢
看电影，她们还喜欢同样[30]的东西，
所以她们的样子[31]一样，衣服一样，
头发[15]一样，水杯一样，开的车一
样，喜欢吃的菜也一样。还有，她们

10

都非常喜欢那个名字叫陈飞的男人。"

　　"她们有不一样的地方吗?"

　　"有。有一个地方她们有一点儿不一样。对对喜欢笑[33]，双双不喜欢笑[33]。双双的脸[19]看起来[16]很冷，她的心[28]也很冷。双双常常不高兴，不高兴的时候她喜欢啃[34]手指甲[35]。对对不啃[34]手指甲[35]，对对很快乐。双双不啃[34]手指甲[35]的时候，没有人知道她是双双还是对对；对对不笑[33]的时候，

5

10

33. 笑 xiào: smile, laugh
34. 啃 kěn: nibble, gnaw
35. 手指甲 shǒuzhǐjiɑ: fingernail

没有人知道她是对对还是双双，她们
的爸爸妈妈也常常不知道。所以，在
她们三岁的时候，她们的爸爸妈妈找
了律师³⁶，留³⁷下了她们的指纹³⁸。"

5 　　"指纹³⁸？"

　　"是的，指纹³⁸。在她们的律师³⁶
那里。"

　　"请您想一想，"李亮又问，"昨天
中午让你早点儿走的那个小姐，她对
10 你笑³³了吗？她啃³⁴手指甲³⁵了没有？"

　　"对，她笑³³了一下，但是很快就
不笑³³了；她笑³³的样子³²也有点儿
冷，不像对对的笑³³，对对笑³³的样
子³¹很好看，所以我想她不是对对。
15 她走进房间³的时候，我看见⁹她像要
啃³⁴手指甲³⁵，但是又没有啃³⁴，所以
我觉得她又不像双双。我现在真不知
道她是双双还是对对了。"

　　"你昨天还看到听到什么了？"王
20 明问。

　　"刚刚³⁹走进房间³的时候，我听

36. 律师 lǜshī: lawyer, attorney
37. 留 liú: remain, stay, keep, save
38. 指纹 zhǐwén: fingerprint
39. 刚刚 gānggāng: just, only; just now

到她们在争吵⁴⁰。"

"争吵⁴⁰? 为什么?"李亮问。

"我不知道她们为什么争吵⁴⁰,但是我想,应该是因为那个叫陈飞的男人,她们在争吵⁴⁰的时候说了陈飞的名字。"

"请说说那个陈飞。"

"那个男人看起来¹⁶不错,"老保姆²⁹说,"我想他有三十多岁,好看、客气、快乐,常常告诉我们一些¹⁸有意思的事。两个月以前,他喜欢双双,是双双的男朋友,常常带双双一起看电影、买东西,还常常给双双写信送礼物。现在,不知道为什么,他变⁴¹了,他跟双双远了,跟对对近了,常常带对对去公园,去游泳,去参加同学的party,也常常给对对写信送礼物。就是说,现在他跟对对好,不跟双双好了。我知道,双双和对对都是第一次爱⁴²一个男人,两个人都非常爱⁴²陈飞,所以,她们应该是因为这个男人争吵⁴⁰。"

---

40. 争吵 zhēngchǎo: quarrel, dispute
41. 变 biàn: change
42. 爱 ài: love

"谢谢你告诉我们这些事。"王明说。

李亮警官[4]又拿出那个本子[22]，在本子[22]上写下刚才听到和看到的事情[23]：

这个红楼里有两个很有钱的孪生[13]姐妹[14]，她们有很多一样的地方：都长得很好看，也长得非常像；她们的头发[16]一样，喜欢的东西、穿的衣服、开的车、爱[42]吃的菜也都一样。所以人们[25]常常不知道谁是姐姐林双双，谁是妹妹[24]林对对。在她们三岁的时候，她们的爸爸妈妈留[37]下了她们的指纹[38]，这些[18]指纹[38]现在在律师[36]那里。

她们不一样的地方是：姐姐双双的心[28]很冷，常常不高兴，她喜欢啃[34]手指甲[35]；妹妹[24]对对是个快乐的人，她常常对人笑[33]，常常帮别人[43]。

两年前，她们的爸爸妈妈死[1]了。今年，这两个孪生[13]姐妹[14]都爱[42]上了一个叫陈飞的男人。两个月前，这个男人是双双的男朋友。现在，他变[41]了，他喜欢对对了，现在是对对的男

---

43. 别人 biérén: other people, others

朋友。昨天中午，她们两个人因为这
个男人争吵[40]过。

　　李亮在本子[22]上还写了这样的话：

　　我们现在还不知道，昨天，也就
是6月8号星期四的中午，死[1]了的那
个小姐是双双还是对对？说死[1]了的人
是对对吧，她为什么在信上写双双的
名字？说死[1]了的人是双双吧，她为什
么死[1]在对对的房间[3]里？为什么用对
对的水杯？还有，她真的是自杀[26]吗？

　　写完这些[18]话，李亮警官[4]对王明警官[4]说："现在，我们知道了一些[18]新的事情[23]，但是还有一些[18]问题，还有一些[18]事情[23]我们不知道。我们去双双和对对的大学吧，看看她们的同学知道什么。"

　　"好吧。"王明很快上了汽车。

　　"喂，李亮，你见你的新女朋友了吗？她怎么样？"在开车的时候，王明笑[33]着问李亮。

　　李亮说："我打算明天晚上和她见面。"

　　"我能看看她的照片吗？"

　　"对不起，我没有。"

"她一定很漂亮吧?"王明又问。

"我的大学同学告诉我,她很漂亮。但是,我想,她的脸[19]一定不会很红。"

"为什么?脸[19]红不好吗?"王明问。 5

"不好。不知道为什么,现在,我看见[9]女人的脸[19]太红,就会想到喝了氰化物[20]的人,想到那个死[1]了的小姐。"李亮说。 10

Want to check your understanding of this part?
Go to the questions on page 55.

4．第三个证人[6]的话

李亮警官[4]跟王明警官[4]开车来到双双和对对的大学。那个大学很远，他们开车走了五十多分钟[5]。大学很大，有很多房子，有的房子很新，有的房子很老，那些[18]很老的房子非常好看。

"真想参观参观大学里这些[18]老房子。"王明说。

"是啊，我也很喜欢这些[18]老房子。我觉得，老房子比新房子有意思。等结案[44]后，我们一起参观吧！现在，我们先工作。"李亮说。

"行！"王明高兴地说。

他们走进一个教室。教室里有一个女老师和二十多个外国学生，外国学生在跟老师学中文。女老师告诉李亮警官[4]和王明警官[4]，她的学生都是外国人，双双和对对不是她的学生，

44. 结案 jié àn: close a case

中国人不用上她的中文课。但是，她
知道双双和对对有个好朋友，她的名
字叫王美美。王美美不上课的时候，
最喜欢去图书馆。有个外国同学也
说，他刚才看见⁹王美美在图书馆复习 5
英文，准备考试。

　　李亮警官⁴和王明警官⁴在大学的
图书馆里找到了王美美。王美美在看
英文书。"啊，她的脸¹⁹怎么也这么
红?!"看见⁹王美美，李亮马上觉得自 10
己²⁷像得了感冒一样，心²⁸里很不舒
服。

"双双和对对都不会自杀²⁶。"王
美美想都没想，就很快地说。

"为什么?"王明问。

"因为双双非常爱⁴²自己²⁷，对对
非常爱⁴²别人⁴³、爱⁴²大家。"

李亮想，王美美说得很对，非常
爱⁴²自己²⁷的人不会自杀²⁶，非常爱⁴²
别人⁴³、爱⁴²大家的人也不会自杀²⁶。

"你认识她们多少年了?"李亮问。

"三年了。我刚上大学就认识了
她们。"

"双双和对对的事你一定知道很
多，请告诉我们，好吗?"王明说。

"双双的心²⁸很冷，不爱⁴²大家。
她对同学和老师都不好，所以她的朋
友很少⁴⁵。今年五月的一天中午，几
个同学在房间³里睡觉，双双跑进来，
她刚刚³⁹游泳回来，觉得房间³里有点
儿热，就马上开了空调⁴⁶，房间³里很
快就变⁴¹得非常冷，有三个睡觉的同
学得了感冒。双双常常做这样的事，
所以同学们都不喜欢她，她的朋友也
很少⁴⁵。"

45. 少 shǎo: few, little, less
46. 空调 kōngtiáo: air-conditioner

22

"对对呢？"李亮问。

"对对对人很好，很爱[42]大家，所以她的朋友很多。那天，对对看见[9]同学们得了感冒，觉得是双双的错，就开车带得了感冒的同学去看病，对对还帮她们买了药，那些[18]药很贵。"

"对对有自己[27]的汽车？"李亮问。

"是的，对对有自己[27]的汽车，是红的 BMW 汽车，非常漂亮。双双也有汽车，也是红的 BMW。那两辆[47]汽

5

10

47. 辆 liàng: a classifier for vehicles

车是她们二十岁生日的时候，爸爸妈妈送给她们的生日礼物。你们知道，她们的爸爸妈妈很有钱，所以给她们买了那样[48]贵的车。坐公共汽车来大

5 学很方便，但是她们很少[45]坐公共汽车。她们常常自己[27]开车到大学来。双双的汽车不让同学们坐。对对跟她不一样，对对常常跟同学、朋友们一起开车去旅行，晚上一起去看电影、

10 买东西，还常常跟大家一起去听音乐。"

---

48. 那样 nàyàng: that kind of, such; in that case

"要快一点儿找到她们的汽车。"
听到这儿，<u>李亮</u>对<u>王明</u>说。

"是的。"<u>王明</u>说。

"<u>双双</u>不爱⁴²大家，可是，她是<u>对
对</u>的姐姐，她爱⁴²她的妹妹²⁴ <u>对对</u>
吗?"<u>李亮</u>问<u>王美美</u>。

"以前，<u>双双</u>爱⁴²<u>对对</u>，因为她们
的爸爸妈妈在外国的时候，飞机出事³²
了，家里只⁴⁹有<u>双双</u>和<u>对对</u>两个人
了。但是，两个月前，<u>双双</u>的男朋友
<u>陈飞</u>变⁴¹了，他不再给<u>双双</u>写信、送
礼物，也不再带<u>双双</u>一起出去看电
影、买东西了;他跟<u>对对</u>好了，常常
带<u>对对</u>一起去公园、去游泳、一起参
加同学的 party，还打算一起去旅行。
从那个时候开始，<u>双双</u>就不爱⁴²<u>对对</u>，
开始恨⁵⁰<u>对对</u>了，因为她觉得，是因
为<u>对对</u>，她没有了<u>陈飞</u>，没有了自
己²⁷爱⁴²的男人，是<u>对对</u>对不起她。"

"认识你很高兴，谢谢你告诉我们
这些¹⁸事。再见!"<u>李亮</u>客气地说。

走出大学的图书馆，<u>李亮</u>拿出本
子²²，写了这些¹⁸话:

5

10

15

20

49. 只 zhǐ: only, just, merely
50. 恨 hèn: hate

现在我们知道：双双和对对很不一样，双双是个只⁴⁹爱⁴²自己²⁷、不爱⁴²大家的人，所以她的朋友很少⁴⁵。对对跟双双不一样。对对爱⁴²别人⁴³，常常想着大家，所以，她的朋友很多。

5 两个月前，因为陈飞变⁴¹了，他跟双双远了，跟对对近了，所以双双开始恨⁵⁰对对。

10 李亮还在本子²²上写了这样的话：

双双和对对都很少⁴⁵坐公共汽车，她们都有红的BMW汽车，那是她们二十岁生日的时候，爸爸妈妈送

15 给她们的生日礼物。

现在，李亮和王明要找到双双和对对的红BMW汽车。

Want to check your understanding of this part?
Go to the questions on page 55–56.

5．第四个证人[6]的话

　　在林双双和林对对住的小区[51]
里，李亮和王明找到了小区[51]的保
安[52]，一个长得很高的男人。李亮和
王明看见[9]他的时候，他准备去吃晚
饭。李亮客气地说："先生，对不起，　　5
我知道你准备去吃晚饭，可是我们
有一些[18]问题，我想你能帮我们。你
应该知道一些[18]我们还不知道的事。
你先告诉我们，再去吃饭，可以吗？"

　　"可以，我正要去吃饭，可是没关　　10
系，"保安[52]说，"晚饭可以晚一点儿
吃。别客气，你们想知道什么事？"

　　"谢谢！"李亮说，"你认识林双双
和林对对吗？就是那两个都开红的
BMW汽车的小姐？"　　15

　　"啊，我知道她们。"保安[52]说。
"那是两个漂亮的小姐，她们是孪生[13]

---

51. 小区 xiǎoqū: residential district
52. 保安 bǎo'ān: security personnel

姐妹 [14]，长得非常像，穿的衣服和头发 [15] 都一样，还有，她们的汽车都是红的 BMW，非常贵的那一种。请看，这辆 [46] 汽车就是她们的。"保安 [51] 说。

李亮和王明看见 [9]，在保安 [52] 后边 [53] 不远，有一辆 [47] 很新、很漂亮的红 BMW 汽车。

"双双的车牌 [54] 号是 865，对对的车牌 [54] 号是 866，因为她们两个人长得太像了，大家常常不知道谁是双双，谁是对对，所以我们保安 [52] 就叫她们'5 号小姐'和'6 号小姐'。"

53. 后边 hòubian: at the back, in the rear, behind
54. 车牌 chēpái: license plate

"请你再想一想，这几天你看见⁹'5号小姐'双双和'6号小姐'对对了吗？"王明问保安⁵²。

"昨天和今天，我都没有看见⁹她们，但是7号，也就是星期三上午，我看见⁹'5号小姐'双双或者⁵⁵'6号小姐'对对开车出去了。"

"开车出去了？你不知道那个开车出去的人是'5号小姐'还是'6号小姐'吗？"李亮问。

"真不知道。我们都知道'5号小姐'双双的脸¹⁹很冷，不爱⁴²笑³³，爱⁴²啃³⁴手指甲³⁵；'6号小姐'对对爱⁴²对别人⁴³笑³³，不爱⁴²啃³⁴手指甲³⁵。但是她们不笑³³、不啃³⁴手指甲³⁵的时候，我们不知道谁是双双，谁是对对。"保安⁵²笑³³着说。

"7号上午，我先看见⁹'5号小姐'双双或者⁵⁵'6号小姐'对对从房子里走出来，天很热，她穿着红衣服，很短，很好看。她没有看我，啃³⁴着手指甲³⁵走到865号车前，我想，她应该是'5号小姐'双双。可是，她在865号车上坐了一会儿，又下来，

55. 或者 huòzhě: or

回到房子里。五分钟[5]后，她又啃[34]着手指甲[35]走出来，这次，她走到866号车前，开着866号车走了。她的车开到我前边[7]的时候，她从车里对我笑[33]了一下。你们知道，'5号小姐'双双没有跟我们保安[52]笑[33]过，'6号小姐'对对没有啃[34]过手指甲[35]，所以，我真的不知道开866号车出去的小姐是双双还是对对。"

"谢谢你，快去吃晚饭吧！"李亮对长得很高的保安[52]说。

李亮又拿出本子[22]，在本子[22]上写了这样的话：

6月7号上午，双双或者[55]对对开着对对的866号车从家里走了。现在，我们要知道，开车走的小姐是双双还是对对？那天她到哪儿去了？

5

"我们应该去机场[56]看看！"王明对李亮说。他们开车很快到了机场[56]。

Want to check your understanding of this part?
Go to the questions on page 56.

56. 机场 jīchǎng: airport

6. 第五个证人[6]的话

　　李亮以前就认识机场[56]的一个警
官，他是李亮大学同学的哥哥。

　　"好久不见，你看起来[16]不错啊！
身体好吧？"李亮笑[33]着说。看见[9]弟
弟的同学李亮来了，机场[56]的警官[4]很
高兴，他帮李亮和王明从很多客人的
名字里找到了林对对，现在，他们知
道林对对是6月7号上午坐飞机去上海
的。在机场[56]，他们还找到了林对对
的866号红BMW汽车。机场[56]有很多
汽车，那里的汽车保安[52]都很忙。

　　"你好！我们能不能问你几个问
题？"

　　"可以。有什么问题，你请说。"
一个保安[52]很客气地说。

　　"这辆[47]红BMW汽车是什么时候
开到这儿的？开车的人是什么样子[31]
的？"

"请你等一下，让我想一想……
啊，我想起来了！开这辆[47]汽车的是
一个小姐，她穿着很短的红衣服，长
得很漂亮，像是个大学生。她是在6
月7号上午10点钟开车到机场[56]来
的。"

李亮问："你看见[9]那个小姐的时
候，她在做什么？你看见[9]她啃[34]手指
甲[35]了吗？她笑[33]了吗？"

汽车保安[52]说："那小姐从车上下
来的时候，我看见[9]她啃[34]着手指甲[35]，
我没有看见[9]那个小姐笑[33]。"

"谢谢你！"王明笑³³着很客气地说。"不客气，"机场⁵⁶的汽车保安⁵²也笑³³着说。

问完了保安⁵²，李亮拿出本子²²来
5　写了下面²¹这些¹⁸话：

现在我们已经知道，6月7号上午10点钟，一个小姐开着866号汽车来到机场⁵⁶，坐飞机去了上海。在坐飞机
10　的客人的名字里，这个小姐写的名字是林对对，不是林双双。但是林对对家小区⁵¹的那个长得很高的保安⁵²和机场⁵⁶的保安⁵²都看见⁹她啃³⁴手指甲³⁵，可是林对对不喜欢啃³⁴手指甲³⁵。

15　那天坐飞机去上海的小姐真的是林对对吗？

"我们应该马上到上海去！"李亮对王明说。

20　"不，是你应该马上到上海去，我应该马上去律师³⁶那里找那些指纹³⁸，我还要知道那个叫陈飞的男人是谁。"王明说。

Want to check your understanding of this part?
Go to the questions on page 56.

7. 第六个证人⁶的话

6月10号上午，李亮走进上海的锦江饭店⁵⁷。

"先生，您好！"一个女服务员⁵⁸对他说。那个女服务员⁵⁸脸¹⁹红红的，李亮看见⁹了就在心²⁸里大叫："这是怎么了？为什么我看见⁹的女人，脸¹⁹都这么红？"

在饭店⁵⁷的客人的名字里，李亮看到有一个是林对对，她的房间³是609号。红脸¹⁹女服务员⁵⁸告诉李亮，十分钟⁵前，这个房间³的小姐刚走，她说要坐飞机回北京。

"请你说说，这个小姐什么时候来饭店⁵⁷的？她来以后⁵⁹做过什么事？说过什么话？"李亮对服务员⁵⁸说。

"这个小姐真有意思。"女服务员⁵⁸

5

10

15

57. 饭店 fàndiàn: hotel
58. 服务员 fúwùyuán: attendant, waiter, waitress
59. 以后 yǐhòu: after, later

35

慢慢地说，"7号中午，她啃[34]着手指甲[35]来到锦江饭店，给了钱，我带她走进房间[3]，她喝了一杯[60]水，几分钟[5]后，她就啃[34]着手指甲[35]走出去了，到昨天上午她才[61]回来，回来的时候她还是啃[34]着手指甲[35]。"

"你是说，这个房间[3]她给了三天的钱，可是从7号中午到现在，她在饭店[57]只[49]住了昨天一个晚上；7号、8号和昨天上午，一共四十多个小时，她都不在饭店[57]里，7号晚上和8号晚上也不住这儿。对吗？"李亮问。

---

60. 杯 bēi: a classifier for cup, glass etc.
61. 才 cái: only, just; not... until

"对，是这样。昨天上午她回来的时候，好像⁶²很累的样子³²，她回房间³以后⁵⁹就没有出来过，我也没有看见⁹她出来吃饭。我想，她那么⁶³长时间一定都在睡觉。十几分钟⁵以前，她拿着东西出来了，她说要坐飞机回北京。我不懂，她为什么在这么贵的饭店⁵⁷开⁶⁴了三天房间³，可是只⁴⁹住了一个晚上？还有，她来的时候和出去的时候都在啃³⁴手指甲³⁵。真是个有意思的小姐！"

"她在饭店⁵⁷的时候，你看见⁹她笑³³过吗？"李亮又问。

"没有，她没有笑³¹过，我只⁴⁹看见⁹她啃³⁴手指甲³⁵。"

服务员⁵⁸说完，带着李亮走进锦江饭店⁵⁷609号房间³。在房间³里，李亮找到了那个小姐的指纹³⁸。

5

10

15

62. 好像 hǎoxiàng: as if, look like, seem
63. 那么 nàme: in that way, then, in that case; so
64. 开 kāi: reserve or pay for (a hotel room)

坐飞机回北京以前，李亮又拿出他的本子[22]，在本子[22]上写了下面[21]这些[18]话：

5　　上海锦江饭店[57]女服务员[58]说：一个小姐用林对对的名字开[64]了三天房间[3]，可是只[49]住了9号一个晚上。那个小姐常常啃[34]手指甲[35]，没有笑[33]过。十几分钟[5]前那个小姐刚走，她说

10　要坐飞机回北京。她真的是妹妹[24]林对对吗？她很像姐姐林双双。

Want to check your understanding of this part?
Go to the questions on page 56–57.

8. 错在哪里

今天是 6 月 10 号。下午，李亮警官[4]和王明警官[4]又开车去了那个像大公园一样的漂亮小区[51]。昨天，也就是 6 月 9 号上午，一个送信的男人在这里看见[9]小区[51]里那个最漂亮的红楼里，有个漂亮的小姐死[1]了。李亮警官[4]和王明警官[4]来到红楼前，在那里等着。他们知道，现在，已经到了结案[44]的时候了。

半小时后，一辆[47]很新的红 BMW 汽车开到红楼前，一个漂亮的小姐走下汽车，她穿着红的短衣服，很好看。

她刚刚[39]打开房子的门[10]，李亮马上问："是林双双吧?"

"是啊!"那小姐说。但是，她的脸[19]马上红了，很快又说："不，我不是林双双，我叫林对对。你是谁?"

李亮拿出警官证[65]，对她说："林双双，我们是警察[66]。我们已经知道，你用氰化物[20]杀[67]死[1]了你的妹妹[24]林对对。"

5   "不，这不是真的！我就是林对对，我没有杀[67]人！我6月7号就到上海旅行去了，我在上海一共住了三天，住在锦江饭店[57]，现在刚刚[39]回北京！"那个小姐大叫着说。

10   "真是这样的吗？"李亮也大叫着问。

"真是这样，我坐飞机去上海，机

65. 警官证 jǐngguānzhèng: police ID
66. 警察 jǐngchá: police
67. 杀 shā: kill

场[56]的人知道，上海锦江饭店[57]的服务员[58]也知道，你们可以去问他们！"

"林双双，你真是个脸[19]冷心[28]也冷的女人。"李亮说，"让我告诉你吧，你听着，有个骗子[68]想拿走你和你妹妹[24]林对对的钱，这个骗子[68]就是陈飞。他以前喜欢你，跟你好，常常给你写信送礼物，带你一起看电影、买东西。两个月前，他变[41]了，他跟你远了，跟你妹妹[24]对对近了，他给对对写信送礼物，带对对去公园、去游泳，还和对对一起参加同学的party。这样，你就觉得是因为你妹妹[24]对对，你没有了男朋友，没有了爱[42]你的人。所以，你恨[50]对对，要杀[67]死[1]对对，让陈飞再爱[42]你。可是，你觉得陈飞现在爱[42]的人是对对，不是你，你就想杀[67]死[1]对对，以后[59]告诉别人[43]你就是对对，你觉得这样陈飞就会再爱[42]你。"

那个小姐说："不，你说的都不是真的！这几天我去上海了，怎么会杀[67]人呢？"

李亮说："不错，6月7号上午，

68. 骗子 piànzi: swindler, cheater

你用你妹妹²⁴林对对的名字坐飞机去了上海。你想让别人⁴³觉得你是对对，所以那天你开着对对的866号汽车去机场，在小区⁵¹还像对对一样，跟保安⁵²笑³³了一下。6月7号中午你到了上海，你啃³⁴着手指甲³⁵，在很贵的锦江饭店⁵⁷开⁶⁴了房间³，你给了钱，但是没有在饭店⁵⁷住，就马上出来了。你坐火车⁶⁹回到了北京。"

李亮说到这里，那个小姐的脸¹⁸开始变⁴¹白⁷⁰了。

李亮说："6月8号上午，你回到了家。你跟对对说，'陈飞是我的，

69. 火车 huǒchē: train
70. 白 bái: white

还⁷¹给我。'你还告诉对对，她不还⁷¹给你陈飞，你就要杀⁶⁷死¹她。但是对对不听你的话，她和你争吵⁴⁰起来。你家的老保姆²⁹来做午饭，她看见⁹你和对对都在家。你对保姆²⁹说，'你今天早点儿走吧，我们有点儿事，要马上回大学去。今天不用做午饭了'。因为你想要让别人⁴³觉得你是对对，所以你又像对对那样⁴⁸，对老保姆²⁹笑³³了一下。可是，因为你的心²⁸很冷，你恨⁵⁰对对，所以你的笑³³不像对对；你想啃³⁴手指甲³⁵，但是想到要让别人⁴³觉得你是对对，就没有啃³⁴。"

71. 还 huán: give back

那个小姐说："你怎么知道一定是我杀[67]了人呢？"

李亮说："老保姆[29]走了。在对对看不见的时候，你拿出氰化物[20]放[72]到她的杯子[17]里。"

那个小姐说："氰化物[20]？我不知道那是什么东西。"

李亮说："看，这就是那个有氰化物[20]的瓶子[73]，瓶子[73]上有你林双双的指纹[38]，我们是在你的汽车里找到这个瓶子[73]的。"

李亮拿出一个小瓶子[73]，那个小姐看了看，"啊"了一下，不说话了。

72. 放 fàng: put, place, add, put in
73. 瓶子 píngzi: bottle, jar

李亮又说："对对喝了一点儿水，很快就死[1]了。你马上写了信，信上说'我很累，我走了'。你还写上了林双双的名字，放[72]到对对的衣服上。你觉得，大家看见[9]信，应该想，死[1]的人是林双双，林双双是自杀[26]的。这样，别人[43]觉得你是对对，陈飞就爱[42]你了。但是，你不知道，在写着林双双名字的信上，有你的指纹[38]。"

说到这里，李亮拿出自己[27]带的杯子[17]，喝了一点儿水以后[59]，他又说："6月8号晚上，你又坐火车[69]去上海，6月9号，也就是昨天上午，你回到了锦江饭店[57]。这几天你累了，昨天在锦江饭店[57]睡了一个下午和一个晚上，今天上午从上海坐飞机回北京，现在刚刚[39]到家。你7号坐飞机去上海，在锦江饭店[57]给了三天的钱，今天又坐飞机从上海回来，你这样做，是想让别人[43]觉得这三天你都在上海玩儿，所以你妹妹[24]不是你杀[67]的。可是，你错了！你说你是对对，不是双双。但是，我在锦江饭店[57]的房间[3]里找到了一些[18]指纹[38]，那些[18]指纹[38]和律师[36]那里的林双双的指纹[38]是一样的。"

那个小姐的脸[19]又红了，她大叫着说："是的！是我杀[67]死[1]了对对，我恨[50]她！因为她，我没有了男朋友，没有了爱[42]……但是，我爱[42]陈飞！"

"林双双啊，林双双，陈飞真的是个骗子[68]。看，这是他的照片。"李亮拿出了陈飞的照片，"他不叫陈飞，以前他的名字叫谢力 (Xiè Lì)。今年2月，他认识了一个有钱的小姐，那个小姐爱[42]上了他，他很快拿走了她爸爸的钱，她爸爸没有钱了，那个小姐

也自杀[26]了……所以，警察[66]都在找他！现在，陈飞又想拿走你们的钱，你做了陈飞想做的事。你杀[67]死[1]了对对，这样，那些钱和房子就都是你一个人的了。你知道吗，他很快就会跟你要钱了！"

"不，不是这样的！我知道陈飞不是骗子[68]，他是个好男人！"他没有跟我要过钱！林双双还是红着脸[19]大叫着说。

这时候，有电话来了。

"对对吗？我是陈飞。你好吗？我很想你！我告诉你一件事：我妈妈病了，病得很重，我明天要坐飞机去看

她，请你帮帮我，借给我 10 万[74] 块钱。我很快就还[71]给你，好吗?"

林双双拿着电话，脸[19]变[41]得很红很红。看到林双双的脸[19]变[41]红了，李
5　　亮想，啊，她怎么也像喝了氰化物[20]一样呢?

林双双没有说什么，放[72]下了电话。

"你看，陈飞开始跟你要钱了，现在你知道他是骗子[68]了吧。但是没关系，几分钟[5]后，他就会坐进警察[66]的
10　　汽车。现在，请你也上我们的汽车吧，'5 号小姐' 林双双!"

李亮说完，带着林双双上了汽车。

Want to check your understanding of this part?
Go to the questions on page 57.

74. 万 wàn: ten thousand

9. 这个小姐脸[19]不红

今天是 6 月 10 号，星期六。晚上，<u>李亮</u>警官[4]换了新衣服，看起来[16]很 cool。大学同学给他介绍了一个女朋友，两天了，<u>李亮</u>还没有见过她呢！那两个孪生[13]姐妹[14]的事很快要结案[44]了，现在他有时间跟女朋友见面了。同学还说，他的新女朋友很漂亮！现在<u>李亮</u>非常高兴。他唱着他喜欢唱的"等着我吧，朋友"，走了出去。公园不太远，不用开汽车，他走了十多分钟[5]就到了。

<u>李亮</u>刚到公园，还没有找地方坐下，一个漂亮的小姐也走了进来。那个小姐高高的，头发[15]很短，穿着白[70]衣服，样子[32]很好看。<u>李亮</u>很快地走过去，笑[33]着说："你好！我是<u>李亮</u>。"那个小姐也笑[33]了笑，说："你好，<u>李亮</u>。"

5

10

15

49

李亮看着那个小姐的脸[19]，很高兴：她的脸[19]很漂亮，但不是红红的！

To check your vocabulary of this reader,
go to the questions on page 57.

To check your global understanding of this reader,
go to the questions on page 58–59.

生词表
Vocabulary list

1	死	sǐ	die
2	地上	dìshang	on the floor
3	房间	fángjiān	room
4	警官	jǐngguān	police officer
5	分钟	fēnzhōng	minute
6	证人	zhèngrén	witness
7	前边	qiánbian	in front
8	走来走去	zǒulái-zǒuqù	pace, walk up and down
9	看见	kàn jiàn	catch sight of, see
10	门	mén	door, gate
11	里边	lǐbian	inside
12	躺	tǎng	lie down
13	孪生	luánshēng	twinborn
14	姐妹	jiěmèi	sisters
15	头发	tóufa	hair (on the head)
16	看起来	kàn qilai	seem, look like
17	杯子	bēizi	cup, glass
18	些	xiē	some, few, several
19	脸	liǎn	face
20	氰化物	qínghuàwù	cyanide, prussiate
21	下面	xiàmian	below, under, underneath
22	本子	běnzi	notebook
23	事情	shìqing	thing, matter
24	妹妹	mèimei	younger sister
25	人们	rénmen	people, the public

26	自杀	zìshā	commit suicide
6 29	自己	zìjǐ	oneself
28	心	xīn	heart, mind
6 29	保姆	bǎomǔ	nanny, housekeeper
30	同样	tóngyàng	same
31	样子	yàngzi	appearance, shape
7 32	出事	chū shì	have an accident
33	笑	xiào	smile, laugh
8 34	啃	kěn	nibble, gnaw
9 35	手指甲	shǒuzhǐjia	fingernail
36	律师	lǜshī	lawyer, attorney
37	留	liú	remain, stay, keep, save
10 38	指纹	zhǐwén	fingerprint
39	刚刚	gānggāng	just, only; just now
11 40	争吵	zhēngchǎo	quarrel, dispute
41	变	biàn	change
42	爱	ài	love
43	别人	biérén	other people, others
12 44	结案	jié àn	close a case
45	少	shǎo	few, little, less
13 46	空调	kōngtiáo	air-conditioner
47	辆	liàng	a classifier for vehicles
48	那样	nàyàng	that kind of, such; in that case
49	只	zhǐ	only, just, merely
14 50	恨	hèn	hate
15 51	小区	xiǎoqū	residential district
52	保安	bǎo'ān	security personnel
53	后边	hòubian	at the back, in the rear, behind
16 54	车牌	chēpái	license plate

55	或者	huòzhě	or
56	机场	jīchǎng	airport
57	饭店	fàndiàn	hotel
58	服务员	fúwùyuán	attendant, waiter, waitress
59	以后	yǐhòu	after, later
60	杯	bēi	a classifier for cup, glass etc.
61	才	cái	only, just; not... until
62	好像	hǎoxiàng	as if, look like, seem
63	那么	nàme	in that way, then, in that case; so
64	开	kāi	reserve or pay for (a hotel room)
65	警官证	jǐngguānzhèng	police ID
66	警察	jǐngchá	police
67	杀	shā	kill
68	骗子	piànzi	swindler, cheater
69	火车	huǒchē	train
70	白	bái	white
71	还	huán	give back
72	放	fàng	put, place, add, put in
73	瓶子	píngzi	bottle, jar
74	万	wàn	ten thousand

练 习
Exercises

1. 有一个小姐死[1]了

   根据故事选择正确答案。 Select the correct answer for each of the questions.

   (1) 谁死[1]了?

       a. 一个小姐   b. 一个男人

   (2) 那个小姐在哪儿?

       a. 房间[3]的地上[2]   b. 在房子外边

   (3) 打电话的人是男的还是女的?

       a. 男的   b. 女的

   (4) 警官[4]对那个打电话的人说了什么?

       a. 你快进去!   b. 在那儿等着,不要让人进去!

   (5) 那天上午还有谁给李亮警官[4]打电话?

       a. 他的女朋友   b. 他的大学同学

   (6) 他的同学说什么了?

       a. 他要跟李亮晚上见面

       b. 他给李亮介绍了一个女朋友

2. 第一个证人[6]的话

   根据故事选择正确答案。 Select the correct answer for each of the questions.

   (1) 打电话的人来这个房子做什么?

       a. 来送信   b. 来找那个小姐

   (2) 住在这个房子里的孪生[13]姐妹[14]叫什么名字?

       a. 姐姐叫双双,妹妹[24]叫对对

b. 姐姐叫对对，妹妹²⁴叫双双

(3) 陈飞两个月前给谁写信送礼物？现在给谁写信送礼物？

　　a. 两个月前给对对，现在给双双

　　b. 两个月前给双双，现在给对对

(4) 死¹了的小姐的脸¹⁹为什么很红？

　　a. 她病了　　　　　b. 她喝了氰化物²⁰

(5) 那个小姐衣服上的信告诉了人们什么？

　　a. 她是自杀²⁶的

　　b. 别人⁴³杀⁶⁷了她

3. 第二个证人⁶的话

下面的说法哪个对，哪个不对？ Mark the correct statements with "T" and the incorrect ones with "F".

(1) 那个五十多岁的女人是孪生¹³姐妹¹⁴的保姆²⁹。　（　　）

(2) 那个小姐死¹在双双的房间³里。　（　　）

(3) 林双双和林对对的爸爸妈妈是在外国死¹的，他们的飞机出事³²了。　（　　）

(4) 律师³⁶有林双双和林对对的指纹³⁸。　（　　）

(5) 双双喜欢笑³³，对对喜欢啃³⁴手指甲³⁵。　（　　）

(6) 林双双和林对对争吵⁴⁰的时候，说了陈飞的名字。（　　）

4. 第三个证人⁶的话

下面的说法哪个对，哪个不对？ Mark the correct statements with "T" and the incorrect ones with "F".

(1) 王美美是林双双和林对对的大学同学，也是她们的朋友。

　（　　）

(2) 王美美觉得那个小姐是自杀²⁶的。　（　　）

(3) 王美美说林对对非常爱[42]自己[27]，林双双非常爱[42]别人[43]。

          （   ）

(4) 林双双和林对对的车都是红的。   （   ）

5. 第四个证人[6]的话

下面的说法哪个对，哪个不对？ Mark the correct statements with "T" and the incorrect ones with "F".

(1) 双双是5号小姐，对对是6号小姐。   （   ）

(2) 6月7号开车出去的小姐没有啃[34]手指甲[35]。   （   ）

(3) 她去机场[56]开的是865号车。   （   ）

(4) 她对保安[52]笑[33]了。   （   ）

6. 第五个证人[6]的话

下面的说法哪个对，哪个不对？ Mark the correct statements with "T" and the incorrect ones with "F".

(1) 机场[56]的一个警官[4]和李亮是大学同学。   （   ）

(2) 机场[56]的汽车保安[52]说，开866号汽车到机场[56]的小姐啃[34]手指甲[35]了。   （   ）

(3) 汽车保安[52]说，那个小姐在机场[56]也笑[33]了。   （   ）

7. 第六个证人[6]的话

下面的说法哪个对，哪个不对？ Mark the correct statements with "T" and the incorrect ones with "F".

(1) 锦江饭店[57]的女服务员[58]说，那天住在609号房间[3]的小姐啃[34]手指甲[35]了。   （   ）

(2) 那个小姐在锦江饭店[57]开[64]了一天房间[3]。   （   ）

(3) 她在那里住了一个晚上。   （   ）

(4) 女服务员⁵⁸说,那个小姐在锦江饭店⁵⁷笑³³过。 （　　）

(5) 李亮在609号房间³里找到了那个小姐的杯子¹⁷。 （　　）

8. 错在哪里

下面的说法哪个对,哪个不对? Mark the correct statements with "T" and the incorrect ones with "F".

(1) 两个警官⁴到那个红楼以前,开BMW的小姐已经回来了。

（　　）

(2) 警官⁴问:"是林双双吧?"那个小姐先说是,后说不是。

（　　）

(3) 警官⁴说,那个小姐从上海第一次是坐火车⁶⁹回的北京。

（　　）

(4) 那个小姐就是林双双,不是林对对。 （　　）

(5) 林双双恨⁵⁰陈飞,因为陈飞是骗子⁶⁸。 （　　）

(6) 林双双杀⁶⁷死¹了妹妹²⁴林对对,因为陈飞现在跟对对好,不

爱⁴²自己²⁷。 （　　）

(7) 林双双借了10万⁷⁴块钱给陈飞。 （　　）

9. 这个小姐脸¹⁹不红

下面的说法哪个对,哪个不对? Mark the correct statements with "T" and the incorrect ones with "F".

(1) 两天了,李亮还没见过新女朋友。 （　　）

(2) 李亮新女朋友穿着红衣服。 （　　）

(3) 李亮的新女朋友脸¹⁹不红。 （　　）

综合理解 Global understanding

1. 下表列出了这个故事的主要情节，但是还不完整，请根据故事内容把每个空填上。The table below gives the plot outline of this story. Fill in the blanks to make the outline complete.

Who When	林双双	警官[4]李亮和别人[43]
6月7号 星期三	上午10点：开车去北京机场[56]。 中午：＿＿＿＿＿＿＿＿＿。 晚上：＿＿＿＿＿＿＿＿＿。	
6月8号 星期四	上午：坐火车[69]回到北京的家里。 中午：＿＿＿＿＿＿＿＿＿。 晚上：＿＿＿＿＿＿＿＿＿。	上午11点： 保姆[29]＿＿＿＿＿＿＿＿＿ ＿＿＿＿＿＿＿＿＿＿＿＿。
6月9号 星期五	上午：＿＿＿＿＿＿＿＿＿。 下午和晚上：＿＿＿＿＿＿＿。	上午11点15分： 送信的男人＿＿＿＿＿＿＿＿ ＿＿＿＿＿＿＿＿＿＿＿＿。 11点15分以后[59]，警官[4]做的事： (1) 在小红楼前面，问送信的男人。 (2) 在林双双家里，＿＿＿＿＿＿ ＿＿＿＿＿＿＿＿＿＿＿。 (3) 在大学，＿＿＿＿＿＿＿＿ ＿＿＿＿＿＿＿＿＿＿＿。 (4) 在小区[51]，＿＿＿＿＿＿＿＿ ＿＿＿＿＿＿＿＿＿＿＿。 (5) 在机场[56]，＿＿＿＿＿＿＿＿ ＿＿＿＿＿＿＿＿＿＿＿。
6月10号 星期六	上午：＿＿＿＿＿＿＿＿＿。 下午：警官[4]在林双双家等她，对她说，是她杀[67]死[1]了妹妹[24]林对对，还告诉她陈飞是一个骗子[68]。	上午：李亮警官[4]在上海。 下午：警官[4]去林双双家，告诉林双双，是她杀[67]死[1]了妹妹[24]林对对，还告诉她陈飞是骗子[68]。 晚上：＿＿＿＿＿＿＿＿＿。

</br>

2. 见了第二个证人以后[59]，王明警官做了下面的笔记，但是他的笔记中有错，请把他的错误找出来并改正。The note below was taken by 王明警官 when he and 李亮 met the second witness. But obviously there are many mistakes in this note. Can you find out the mistakes and correct them?

这个红楼里有两个孪生[13]姐妹[14]，她们很有钱，长的样子[31]一样，都非常好看，但是她们喜欢的东西不一样。她们买的东西不一样，穿的衣服不一样，头发[15]也不一样。姐姐叫林对对，她喜欢啃[34]手指甲[35]；她的心[28]很冷，常常不高兴。妹妹[24]林双双很热心[28]，她爱[42]别人[43]，她常常对别人[43]笑[33]。林对对不啃[34]手指甲[35]的时候，没有人知道她是对对还是双双，她们的保姆[29]也不知道。所以，在她们一岁的时候，她们的爸爸妈妈留[37]下了她们的指纹[38]。现在，这些[18]指纹[38]在保安[52]那里。

</br>

练习答案

Answer keys to the exercises

1. 有一个小姐死[1]了
   (1) a   (2) a   (3) a   (4) b   (5) b   (6) b

2. 第一个证人[6]的话
   (1) a   (2) a   (3) b   (4) b   (5) a

3. 第二个证人[6]的话
   (1) T   (2) F   (3) T   (4) T   (5) F   (6) T

4. 第三个证人[6]的话
   (1) T   (2) F   (3) F   (4) T

5. 第四个证人[6]的话
   (1) T   (2) F   (3) F   (4) T

6. 第五个证人[6]的话
   (1) F   (2) T   (3) F

7. 第六个证人[6]的话
   (1) T   (2) F   (3) T   (4) F   (5) F

8. 错在哪里
   (1) F   (2) T   (3) T   (4) T   (5) F
   (6) T   (7) F

9. 这个小姐脸[19]不红
   (1) T   (2) F   (3) T

综合理解 Global understanding

1.

Who / When	林双双	警官[4]李亮和别人[43]
6月7号 星期三	上午10点:开车去北京机场[56]。 中午:坐飞机到上海,在锦江饭店开[64]了房间[3]。 晚上:坐火车[69]回北京。	
6月8号 星期四	上午:坐火车[69]回到北京的家里。 中午:杀[67]死[1]了妹妹[24]林对对。 晚上:坐火车[69]去上海。	上午11点: 保姆[29]来给双双和对对做午饭,她听见双双和对对在争吵[40]。
6月9号 星期五	上午:到了上海锦江饭店[57]。 下午和晚上:在锦江饭店[57]睡觉。	上午11点15分: 送信的男人看到一个小姐死[1]了,她躺[12]在房间[3]的地上[2]。 11点15分以后[59],警官[4]做的事: (1)在小红楼前面,问送信的男人。 (2)在林双双家里,问保姆[29]。 (3)在大学,问王美美。 (4)在小区[51],问高个子保安[52]。 (5)在机场[56],问机场的保安[52]。
6月10号 星期六	上午:从上海坐飞机回到北京。 下午:警官[4]在林双双家等她,对她说,是她杀[67]死[1]了妹妹[24]林对对,还告诉她陈飞是一个骗子[68]。	上午:李亮警官[4]在上海。 下午:警官[4]去林双双家,告诉林双双,是她杀[67]死[1]了妹妹[24]林对对,还告诉她陈飞是骗子[68]。 晚上:李亮在公园跟女朋友见面。

2.

　　这个红楼里有两个孪生[13]姐妹[14]，她们很有钱，长的样子[31]一样，都非常好看，但是她们喜欢的东西<u>不一样</u>(一样)。她们买的东西<u>不一样</u>(一样)，穿的衣服<u>不一样</u>(一样)，头发[15]也<u>不一样</u>(一样)。姐姐叫<u>林对对</u>(林双双)，她喜欢啃[34]手指甲[35]；她的心[28]很冷，常常不高兴。妹妹[24]<u>林双双</u>(林对对)很热心[28]，她爱[42]别人[43]，常常对别人[43]笑[33]。<u>林对对</u>(林双双)不啃[34]手指甲[35]的时候，没有人知道她是对对还是双双，她们的<u>保姆</u>[29](爸爸妈妈)也不知道。所以，在她们<u>一岁</u>(三岁)的时候，她们的爸爸妈妈留[37]下了她们的指纹[38]。现在，这些[18]指纹[38]在<u>保安</u>[52](律师[36])那里。

为所有中文学习者(包括华裔子弟)编写的
第一套系列化、成规模、原创性的大型分级
轻松泛读丛书

"汉语风"(*Chinese Breeze*)分级系列读物简介

"汉语风"(*Chinese Breeze*)是一套大型中文分级泛读系列丛书。这套丛书以"学习者通过轻松、广泛的阅读提高语言的熟练程度,培养语感,增强对中文的兴趣和学习自信心"为基本理念,根据难度分为8个等级,每一级6—8册,共近60册,每册8,000至30,000字。丛书的读者对象为中文水平从初级(大致掌握300个常用词)一直到高级(掌握3,000—4,500个常用词)的大学生和中学生(包括修美国AP课程的学生),以及其他中文学习者。

"汉语风"分级读物在设计和创作上有以下九个主要特点:

一、等级完备,方便选择。精心设计的8个语言等级,能满足不同程度的中文学习者的需要,使他们都能找到适合自己语言水平的读物。8个等级的读物所使用的基本词汇数目如下:

第1级:300 基本词	第5级:1,500 基本词
第2级:500 基本词	第6级:2,100 基本词
第3级:750 基本词	第7级:3,000 基本词
第4级:1,100 基本词	第8级:4,500 基本词

为了选择适合自己的读物,读者可以先看看读物封底的故事介绍,如果能读懂大意,说明有能力读那本读物。如果读不懂,说明那本读物对你太难,应选择低一级的。读懂故事介绍以后,再看一下书后的生词总表,如果大部分生词都认识,说明那本读物对你太容易,应试着阅读更高一级的读物。

二、题材广泛,随意选读。丛书的内容和话题是青少年学生所喜欢的侦探历险、情感恋爱、社会风情、传记写实、科幻恐怖、神话传说等等。学习者可以根据自己的兴趣爱好进行选择,享受阅读的乐趣。

三、词汇实用,反复重现。各等级读物所选用的基础词语是该等级的学习者在中文交际中最需要最常用的。为研制"汉语风"各等级的基础词

表,"汉语风"工程首先建立了两个语料库:一个是大规模的当代中文书面语和口语语料库,一个是以世界上不同地区有代表性的40余套中文教材为基础的教材语言库。然后根据不同的交际语域和使用语体对语料样本进行分层标注,再根据语言学习的基本阶程对语料样本分别进行分层统计和综合统计,最后得出符合不同学习阶程需要的不同的词汇使用度表,以此作为"汉语风"等级词表的基础。此外,"汉语风"等级词表还参考了美国、英国等国和中国大陆、台湾、香港等地所建的10余个当代中文语料库的词语统计结果。以全新的理念和方法研制的"汉语风"分级基础词表,力求既具有较高的交际实用性,也能与学生所用的教材保持高度的相关性。此外,"汉语风"的各级基础语料在读物中都通过不同的语境反复出现,以巩固记忆,促进语言的学习。

四、易读易懂,生词率低。"汉语风"严格控制读物的词汇分布、语法难度、情节开展和文化负荷,使读物易读易懂。在较初级的读物中,生词的密度严格控制在不构成理解障碍的1.5%到2%之间,而且每个生词(本级基础词语之外的词)在一本读物中初次出现的当页用脚注做出简明注释,并在以后每次出现时都用相同的索引序号进行通篇索引,篇末还附有生词总索引,以方便学生查找,帮助理解。

五、作家原创,情节有趣。"汉语风"的故事以原创作品为主,多数读物由专业作家为本套丛书专门创作。各篇读物力求故事新颖有趣,情节符合中文学习者的阅读兴趣。丛书中也包括少量改写的作品,改写也由专业作家进行,改写的原作一般都特点鲜明、故事性强,通过改写降低语言难度,使之适合该等级读者阅读。

六、语言自然,地道有味。读物以真实自然的语言写作,不仅避免了一般中文教材语言的枯燥和"教师腔",还力求鲜活地道。

七、插图丰富,版式清新。读物在文本中配有丰富的、与情节内容自然融合的插图,既帮助理解,也刺激阅读。读物的版式设计清新大方,富有情趣。

八、练习形式多样,附有习题答案。读物设计了不同形式的练习以促进学习者对读物的多层次理解;所有习题都在书后附有答案,以方便查对,利于学习。

九、配有录音,两种语速选择。各册读物所附的故事录音(MP3格式),有正常语速和慢速两种语速选择,学习者可以通过听的方式轻松学习、享受听故事的愉悦。故事录音可通过扫描封底的二维码获得,也可通过网址http://www.pup.cn/dl/newsmore.cfm?sSnom=d203下载。

ABOUT *Hànyǔ Fēng* (*Chinese Breeze*)

Hànyǔ Fēng (*Chinese Breeze*) is a large and innovative Chinese graded reader series which offers nearly 60 titles of enjoyable stories at eight language levels. It is designed for college and secondary school Chinese language learners from beginning to advanced levels (including AP Chinese students), offering them a new opportunity to read for pleasure and simultaneously developing real fluency, building confidence, and increasing motivation for Chinese learning. *Hànyǔ Fēng* has the following main features:

☆ Eight carefully graded levels increasing from 8,000 to 30,000 characters in length to suit the reading competence of first through fourth-year Chinese students:

Level 1: 300 base words	Level 5: 1,500 base words
Level 2: 500 base words	Level 6: 2,100 base words
Level 3: 750 base words	Level 7: 3,000 base words
Level 4: 1,100 base words	Level 8: 4,500 base words

To check if a reader is at one's reading level, a learner can first try to read the introduction of the story on the back cover. If the introduction is comprehensible, the leaner will be able to understand the story. Otherwise the learner should start from a lower level reader. To check whether a reader is too easy, the learner can skim the Vocabulary (new words) Index at the end of the text. If most of the words on the new word list are familiar to the learner, then she/ he should try a higher level reader.

☆ Wide choice of topics, including detective, adventure, romance, fantasy, science fiction, society, biography, mythology, horror, etc. to meet the diverse interests of both adult and young adult learners.

☆ Careful selection of the most useful vocabulary for real life communication in modern standard Chinese. The base vocabulary used for writing each level was generated from sophisticated computational analyses of very large written and spoken Chinese corpora as well as a language databank of over 40 commonly used or representative Chinese textbooks in different countries.

☆ Controlled distribution of vocabulary and grammar as well as the deployment of story plots and cultural references for easy reading and efficient learning, and highly recycled base words in various contexts at each level to maximize language development.

☆ Easy to understand, low new word density, and convenient new word glosses and indexes. In lower level readers, new word density is strictly limited to 1.5% to 2%. All new words are conveniently glossed with footnotes upon first appearance and also fully indexed throughout the texts as well as at the end of the text.

☆ Mostly original stories providing fresh and exciting material for Chinese learners (and even native Chinese speakers).

☆ Authentic and engaging language crafted by professional writers teamed with pedagogical experts.

☆ Fully illustrated texts with appealing layouts that facilitate understanding and increase enjoyment.

☆ Including a variety of activities to stimulate students' interaction with the text and answer keys to help check for detailed and global understanding.

☆ Audio files in MP3 format with two speed choices (normal and slow) accompanying each title for convenient auditory learning. Scan the QR code on the backcover, or visit the website http://www.pup.cn/dl/newsmore.cfm?sSnom=d203 to download the audio files.

"汉语风"系列读物其他分册
Other *Chinese Breeze* titles

　　"汉语风"全套共8级近60册,自2007年11月起由北京大学出版社陆续出版。下面是已经出版或近期即将出版的各册书目。请访问北京大学出版社网站(www.pup.cn)关注最新的出版动态。

　　Hànyǔ Fēng (*Chinese Breeze*) series consists of nearly 60 titles at eight language levels. They have been published in succession since November 2007 by Peking University Press. For most recently released titles, please visit the Peking University Press website at www.pup.cn.

第1级:300词级
Level 1: 300 Word Level

两个想上天的孩子
Two Children Seeking the Joy Bridge

"叔叔,在哪里买飞机票?"

"小朋友,你们为什么来买飞机票? 要去旅行吗?"

"不是。""我们要到天上去。"

……

　　这两个要买飞机票的孩子,一个7岁,一个8岁。没有人知道,他们为什么想上天。这两个孩子也不知道,在他们出来以后,有人给他们的家里打电话,让他们的爸爸妈妈拿钱去换他们呢……

"Sir, where is the air-ticket office?"

"You two kids come to buy air-tickets? Are you gonna travel somewhere?"

"Nope.""We just wanna go up to the Joy Bridge."

"The Joy Bridge?"

...

Of the two children at the airport to buy air-tickets, one is 7 and the other is 8. Beyond their wildest imaginings, after they ran away, their parents were called by some crooks who demanded a ransom to get them back...

67

我一定要找到她……
I Really Want to Find Her...

那个女孩儿太漂亮了，戴伟、杰夫和秋田看到了她的照片，都要去找她！照片是老师死前给他们的，可是照片上的中国女孩儿在哪儿？他们都不知道。最后，他们到中国是怎么找到那个女孩儿的？女孩儿又和他们说了什么？

She is really beautiful. Just one look at her photo and three guys, Dai-wei, Jie-fu and Qiu-tian, are all determined to find her! The photo was given to them by their professor before he died. And nobody knows where in China the girl is. How can the guys find her? And what happens when they finally see her?

我可以请你跳舞吗？
Can I Dance with You?

一个在银行工作的男人，跟他喜欢的女孩子刚认识，可是很多警察来找他，要带他走，因为银行里的一千万块钱不见了，有人说是他拿走的。

但是，拿那些钱的不是他，他知道是谁拿的。可是，他能找到证据吗？这真太难了。还有，以后他还能和那个女孩子见面吗？

A smart young man suddenly gets into big trouble. He just fell in love with a pretty girl, but now the police come and want to arrest him. The bank he works for lost 10 million dollars, and the police list him as a suspect.

Of course he is not the robber! He even knows who did it. But can he find evidence to prove it to the police? It's all just too much. Also, will he be able to see his girlfriend again?

向左向右
Left and Right: The Conjoined Brothers

向左和向右是两个男孩子的名字，爸爸妈妈也不知道向左是哥哥还是向右是哥哥，因为他们连在一起，是一起出生的连体人。他们每天都一起吃，一起住，一起玩儿。他们常常都很快乐。有时候，弟弟病了，哥哥帮他吃药，弟弟的病就好了。但是，学校上课的时候，他们在一起就不方便了……

Left and Right are two brothers. Even their parents don't know who is older and who is younger, as they are Siamese twins. They must do everything together. They play together, eat together, and sleep together. Most of the time they enjoy their lives and are very happy. When one was sick, the other helped his brother take his medicine and he got better. However, it's no fun anymore when they sit in class together but one brother dislikes the other's subjects...

你最喜欢谁？
Whom Do You Like More?

谢红去了外国，她是方新喜欢的人，可是方新不想去外国，因为他要在中关村做他喜欢的工作。小月每天来看方新，她是喜欢方新、也能帮方新的人，可是方新还是想着谢红。方新真不知道应该怎么办……

Xie Hong, Fang Xin's true love, has gone abroad to fulfill her dream. But Fang Xin only wants to stay in Zhongguancun in Beijing doing work that he enjoys. Xiao-yue comes to visit Fang Xin every day. She is the one who really understands Fang Xin. She loves him and can offer him the help that he badly needs. But only Xie Hong is in Fang Xin's mind. What should Fang Xin do? He seems to be losing his way in life...